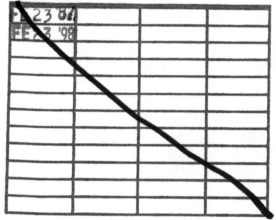

POWER
of the
PRESIDENCY

POWER
of the
PRESIDENCY

James L. Fisher

AMERICAN COUNCIL ON • MACMILLAN PUBLISHING
EDUCATION   COMPANY

NEW YORK

Collier Macmillan Publishers

LONDON

Macmillan Publishing Company
866 Third Avenue, New York, N.Y. 10022

Collier Macmillan Canada, Inc.

Library of Congress Catalog Card Number: 83–15150

Printed in the United States of America

printing number
    3 4 5 6 7 8 9 10

Library of Congress Cataloging in Publication Data

Fisher, James L.
  Power of the presidency.

  Bibliography: p.
  Includes index.
  1. College presidents—United States. 2. Universities
and colleges—United States—Administration. I. Title.
LB2341.F496 1984   378′.111   83–15150
ISBN 0-02-910520-X

This book is dedicated to my mother and father and to Robert Gehlmann Bone, the most naturally charismatic president I have known.

Contents

Preface

This book is for college and university presidents, new and experienced, and for those who would be presidents. Although loosely rooted in research, it is not for scholars; it is for those who work daily in the reality of the college and university marketplaces—on and off campus. The chapters on college and university constituent groups were written with the research in mind, but the application certainly is not always specific or definite. It is for those who must attract the attention and inspire the support of such diverse constituencies as faculty members and trustees, students and newspaper reporters, conservatives and liberals, church leaders and politicians. I hope it will add something of value to the limited literature available on one of the most important positions in our society—the college presidency. Perhaps it will encourage other, more sophisticated research and scholarship efforts on the subject of the effective college presidency.

There was nothing like this available for me in 1969 when I became a college president. I tried to be as good as what I had seen and read. I even attended a three-day conference on how to be a president. Fortunately, I had served under a remarkable president, Robert G. Bone; I was able to watch another, Martin D. Jenkins, during my first and his last presidential years; and, throughout my tenure, I had the extraordinary example of Father Theodore Hesburgh at Notre Dame. But what I read was, for the most part, descriptive or prescriptive with only personal documentation; while it was sometimes inspiring, the literature made little attempt to justify action through evidence. Some of the material was interesting and helpful, but, for the most part, I had to go it alone. It would have been invaluable to have had a reasonably objective and specific guide against which I could measure my presidential inclinations; a guide to accept or to reject, but at least to help me measure. There was nothing. The Prince was too calculating; The New Testament, though helpful, was too personal; and the volumes on management and systems were too impersonal and impractical.

About halfway through my presidential course, I vowed to write one day a guide for presidents that would not only be reasonably objective but also specific and, therefore, undoubtedly controversial. After all, years ago, I had been educated in the field, or at least sufficiently to know of the importance of such research to the presidency. I had experienced the presidency for long enough—almost ten years—to know what it was like. And I had always felt reservations about those who give advice about serving in a leadership position without first having had the experience. I wanted to write a "how to" book based on at least a bit more than personal experience, knowing nonetheless that experience would be a most important ingredient, for it might grant the strength to withstand that academic test of equivocation and complexity. I wanted to write of things usually reserved for the halls of professional meetings and for the perhaps unwritten thoughts of some who have published on the subject. I wanted to write of the questions that are too "dumb" to be asked by the "sophisticated," yet whose answers can illuminate the course for many. I wanted to write for that president who was as scared and as happy as I was when I first walked into that presidential office.

This, then, is the book I resolved to write. It is an effort to present and review briefly the significant research on leadership and power and to discuss each presidential constituency in that light and in the light of my experience. These constituencies include the faculty, staff, students, the influence/benefactor hierarchy, politicians, public figures, the community and general public, bureaucrats, the media, trustees, and alumni. They are presented in relation to such presidential activities as administration, governance, speaking, and personal relationships. I do not pretend that the presentations are completely objective; indeed, I believe that leadership is an art as well as a science, and that an artistic endeavor, if analyzed too closely, can be lost. One must not become so conscious of the detail that spontaneity is squelched. But I have, throughout, attempted to bear in mind the research as well as personal experience in office. The reader will determine how well I have combined the two.

I hope that experienced presidents will find it both helpful as well as amusing, and that new presidents will find it a worthwhile addition to their libraries on the presidency. The presentation is strong by design. Those who know me know that, while I did not always win and I certainly made mistakes, I believed in a strong and assertive presidency. Perhaps it is only natural for one to seek justification through research. Although I could write more than I was, I could not write less than I tried to be. I also believe that strong presidencies will be the imperative of the next decades in higher education. But I do not suggest that there are not effective presidential styles other than the ones encouraged in this book.

I must also stress here the fundamental importance in all presidential behavior of morality, sincerity, decency, respect for others, personal goodness, and true caring. If these humanistic characteristics do not shine through in a president's behavior, no application of presidential method or style will work. The president must maintain complete fidelity in his or her relationships with all individuals. I was best able to determine the extent to which I did this by facing myself each morning in the bathroom mirror. I looked at that unfreshened face, and asked myself whether what I was doing was in the best interest of the people I served—one at a time. And each morning, when I walked into the administration building, I would chuckle to myself as I wondered how in the world this ever happened to me. I know that I was no more confident, no wiser, no better educated, and certainly no better than most of the people I was expected to lead. But, by the time I had walked to the second floor where my office was, I was the president again, and I reveled in the job.

I will cite several books that were of special value to me:

Handbook of Leadership by Ralph Stogdill; *Handbook of Political Psychology* by Jeanne N. Knutson; *The Powerholders* by David Kipnis; *Power in Organizations* by Jeffrey Pfeffer; *The Craft of Power* by R. G. H. Siu; and *Presidential Power* by Richard E. Neustadt. There were others, but none so helpful as these.

The first chapter sets the scene. It discusses the problems and the importance of the college presidency. People appointed to presidencies are almost invariably from more restricted backgrounds. Yet they are expected immediately to be consummate masters of leadership and management. Because of their background and a lack of understanding or an appreciation of tested techniques of leadership and power, many presidents are less effective than they might be. The chapter includes several examples of presidential mistakes, and then makes a case for the college and university presidents' knowing and using tested concepts of leadership and power.

The second chapter considers leadership in higher education today, and presents a brief review of the research on leadership. Today, effective leaders are characterized by a strong drive for responsibility, vigor (or the appearance of vigor), persistence, a willingness to take chances, originality, humor, social initiative, self-confidence, decisiveness, a sense of identity, personal style, a capacity to organize, action, and a willingness to absorb the stress of others.

Chapter 3 reviews the research on power and assumes that all attempts to influence fall under one of five power rubrics. Those five forms of power are, in ascending order of their significance to college presidents: coercive, reward, legitimate, expert, and charismatic. By far, the most effective forms of power for college and university presidents are charismatic and expert, with charismatic power clearly the most significant. Chapter 3 discusses the nature of charismatic power and its prime ingredient, "distance."

The subject of Chapter 4 is the charismatic presidency. From this point on, it is important for the reader to bear in mind that the material is only *loosely* rooted in research. I included documentation where I considered it appropriate and found it available. But much of the interpretation is subjective, based on my impressions from the research and my personal experience in the presidency. I advise the college president to act like a president and to accept the appointments and trappings of office with as much equanimity as possible. He or she also must exploit ethically every occasion to advance the importance and influence of the presidential office. The following are discussed from a charismatic perspective: speaking engagements; ceremonies; confrontations; parties; on- and off-campus adversaries; administrative organization; student, staff, and faculty relations; the importance of a presidential mission; the value of conflict; the role of the spouse and other personal relationships; loneliness; and the importance of superior associates and a good assistant.

Chapter 5 opens the discussion of specific presidential constituencies and the relative value of the various power forms discussed in Chapter 3. This presents the role of the president and the administration. The basic assumption here is twofold: that the administration must be viewed as mission oriented, dynamic, and enlightened; and that all administrators have three choices—they agree with the president, change the president's mind, or resign. There is also a discussion of the importance and nature of structure, delegation, competence, and loyalty. In addition, the chapter talks about the danger of appointing an executive vice president and, assuming this, the nature and role of an officially unnamed but effectively performing number two officer, the academic vice president or principal academic dean.

Chapter 6 covers the role of the president and institutional governance. After first establishing the rationale for faculty and student participation in the governance process, this chapter discusses the importance of the president as the final authority in all matters at the institution. It emphasizes the importance of a governing board investing in the president virtually all of the authority for campus decision making. From this base of authority, the president can then both delegate responsibility and grant privileges without being compromised by undue administrative involvement from off-campus authorities. Also considered in the chapter are collective bargaining, presidential participation in campus governance meetings, and, for public institutions, the role of state systems.

Chapter 7 covers the relationship between the president and the faculty. In this relationship, there is respect for the primacy of the faculty in their disciplines as well as for their right to participate in shaping institutional policy. At the same time, the president preserves and maintains final responsibility and authority. Included are discussions of: the role of faculty organizations and relationships with their leaders; the value of informal contacts; the use of small-group sessions and orientation programs; faculty meetings; attendance at retirement functions, funerals, and other special personal events in the lives of staff, students, and others; the effectiveness of the "intellectual" president; and close friendships with members of the faculty.

The eighth chapter, on students and the president, emphasizes the fundamental importance of good student relations to an effective presidency. Assuming that the best interests of the individual student should be the prime criterion against which a president weighs every decision, it talks about various areas of student contact. These include: orientation; residence hall visits; student leaders; student office hours; formal and informal campus appearances; student protests; and the role and characteristics of the chief student personnel officer.

Chapter 9 centers on the president's external constituencies. After assuming that too many presidents pay too little attention to external affairs, this chapter suggests ways that the president can be more effective in dealing with persons of influence and potential benefactors. It mentions a number of points, including: formal and informal behavior; the kinds of activities in which a president should normally be engaged; the role of directness; the importance of presidential trappings; off-campus speeches; the importance of appearing highly energetic; the controversial president; being an expert; the importance and role of skilled professionals in public relations and development; the need to remember that, so long as you are president, you are the institution; working with your landed aristocracy; dress and comportment; entertainment; and one-on-one sessions with important persons.

Chapter 10 attempts to apply the literature of power to the role of the president with politicians, public figures, and bureaucrats. It assumes that the key to the process is the president's willingness and ability to cultivate the persons on whom the public figure depends—the grass-roots organizations, places, and people. This means the president must work at home to be effective in the seat of government. And, to the extent possible, the president should become a public figure. In effect, he or she must compete in the same arena as those who must be influenced. The chapter also focuses on the nature of politicians, bureaucrats, and other public figures, and cites telling examples.

The news media are discussed in Chapter 11. It advises presidents that this is the one area that is rarely affected by charisma. They must therefore rely almost exclusively on expert power. While the media may often distort and confuse, they are nonetheless largely responsible for developing whatever external charisma the president has. The president must be willing to take chances. There are discussions of the essential role of public-relations professionals; when and where to speak; the nature of news reporters, feature and editorial writers, publishers, and radio and television station managers; becoming a media personality; the do's and don'ts of college and university publications; and the importance of not taking your public image too seriously.

Chapter 12 presents the relationships between the president and trustees. It advises the president about how to relate with trustees in both the public and the private sectors, and discusses the differences between the two. There is also consideration of: presentations to the governing board; the role of other staff; fund raising with and by the board; the role and nature of the development officer; how much trustees should know; the appointment of trustees; the education of trustees; personal relationships with trustees; trustees and the administration of the institution; private foundations in public institutions; trustee disagreements; trustees and the media; and the value of executive board sessions.

Chapter 13 speaks of the president and the alumni and the temptation for presidents to take alumni support for granted. It is assumed that without a strong and enthusiastic base of alumni support, the president is bound to be less effective, and most will not continue long in office. This chapter also covers: the nature of alumni; communicating with alumni; dependent and independent alumni associations; the role and function of alumni professionals; alumni boards; and speaking to alumni groups.

The last chapter, Chapter 14, is a review of material discussed in all of the preceding chapters coupled with concluding reflections and observations about the presidency.

Acknowledgments

I must pay my respect and appreciation to those who have read, edited, and discussed parts of this manuscript: Kenneth A. Shaw, Chancellor, Southern Illinois University; Paul Wisdom, Vice President, Lafayette College; David E. Sweet, President, Rhode Island College; Homer Martin, M.D., Louisville, Kentucky; William I. Ihlanfeldt, Vice President, Northwestern University; Robert G. Forman, Executive Director, University of Michigan Alumni Association; Colette M. Seiple, Assistant Chancellor, University of California at Santa Cruz; H. Sargent Whittier, Jr., Vice President, St. Lawrence University; William Carpenter, Vice President, PPG Industries Foundation; Robert L. Gale, President, Association of Governing Boards of Colleges and Universities; Gary H. Quehl, President, Council of Independent Colleges; Allan W. Ostar, President, American Association of State Colleges and Universities; Tom Clarkson, former Director of College Relations, Des Moines Area Community College; Jacquelyn A. Mattfeld, former President of Barnard College; Arthur E. Ciervo, Director of Public Information and Relations, Pennsylvania State University; Robert A. Reichley, Vice President, Brown University; Warren Heemann, Vice President, Georgia Institute of Technology; James E. Vermette, former President, University of Illinois Alumni Association; William H. Marumoto, President, The Interface Group Ltd. in Washington, D.C. and Los Angeles; and to my extraordinary associate, Virginia Carter Smith, who read, discussed, and edited the entire manuscript—many times. And a special thank you to the PPG Industries Foundation, whose thoughtful and generous grant made it possible for this book to be written in good conscience.

I commend and thank my good and long-suffering associates during my tenure as a university president: Buzz Shaw, Paul Wisdom, Wayne Schelle, Dick Gillespie, Charles Haslup, John Wighton, Joan Fisher, Joe Cox, Dorothy Siegel, Annette Flower, Tracy Miller, Thomas Knox, George Pruitt, and Gil Brungardt; and my able and respected predecessor, Earle Taylor Hawkins. My appreciation to these faculty, students, and alumni: John Carter Mathews, Hank Muma, Mitch Kerr, Rick Neidig, Blaine Taylor, Don Craver, Quenton Thompson, Ruth Drucker, Dean Esslinger, Mark Whitman, Conrad Herrling, Art Madden, Bucky Kimmet, Rick Danoff, Jean Hoppenfeld, David Nevins, Charlie Johnson, Ann Marie Lowe, Kathy Brooks, Doug Martin, Pat Plante, Carroll Rankin, Tom Supenski, Armin Mruck; and to my two "friend mistakes," Vince Angotti and Mike Mahoney, who never abused the relationship. And to all trustees, of course, my respect, and my special admiration to Edgar Berman, the most courageous trustee I knew, a friend who was always there; Victor Frenkil, Bob Watts, Matt DeVito, and Elaine Davis. And my deep appreciation to Bob and Emily DiCicco, Frank Roberts, Mel Berger, Herb and Sue Garten, Al and Bobbie Burke, Jim Nolan, Bill and Mike Flynn, Asa and Sayde Sklar, Austin and Helen Tydings, Francis Knott, Merrill Rief, Blair Lee, John Arnick, Joe Pokorney, Bill Perkins, Jack and Janet Tolbert, Ray Tomkins, Howard and Joan Head, Arthur and Rosie Kramer, Don and Mary Belle Grempler, Jerry, Patti, and Bill Gaudreau, Naz, Johnny "D," and Mrs. Souris . . . and many, many others. I must also thank my assistant, Vivienne Lee, and my secretary, Kathy Yealdhall, both of whom did more work on this volume than I will ever admit. Special thanks also to Kathi Weidenhammer and Barbara McKenna. And for my wife Joan, a formal word of appreciation for her astute advice and constant inspiration.

CHAPTER 1

In the Spirit of St. Simone

An institution is the lengthened shadow of one person.
Ralph Waldo Emerson

Power tends to corrupt, and absolute power corrupts absolutely.
Lord Acton, 1887

Absolute power is OK, if you're careful.
Julius Caesar
(loosely translated from the Latin)

THERE IS A COMMENT attributed to a man named Simone that relates to the college presidency. Simone, an early Christian ascetic, felt the need to demonstrate dramatically to others that the then popular and easy Christianity was not the essence of the faith. In order to do so, Simone erected a sixty-foot tower topped by a platform. For twenty years he stayed up there, preaching to the multitudes who came to observe the spectacle. Simone was so effective from that platform that the Roman Catholic Church made him a saint. It is reported that, after twenty years, St. Simone said about his experience, "The most difficult part was getting on top of the platform."

Most college and university presidents would probably agree that the most difficult aspect of the presidency is not the climb up that tower—securing an appointment—but getting onto the platform and staying firmly put. The platform was Simone's way of creating an aura of distance and mystery about his person, a medium through which his message could be more powerfully delivered. The president also has to create a platform from which to lead his or her institution effectively. That platform or medium is a powerful presidential image.

Need for More Knowledge about the Presidency

Few college or university presidents have sufficient formal knowledge of the legitimate and tested techniques of leadership and power derived from research, and too few realize that these techniques are applicable to a more effective presidency.* Yes, few would have become presidents without a desire for power, but most do not know enough about its nature or use and are, therefore, less effective than they might be. Presidents often fail to understand the value of the presidential position—the platform atop the tower—to their ability to accomplish legitimate and essential institutional goals. As a result, many fall short of their purpose and do not understand why.

To many incumbents the presidency resembles the greased pole at the Italian Fair in Baltimore each year; like the hearty spirits who try to climb that pole, presidents ascend with vigor and descend precipitously. Presidents know how important the office is, but are at first ignorant of its price, and later are unsure they are willing to pay it. The presidency offers a heady combination of confidence and uncertainty. This is why the job is such an enigma, such a delightfully bewildering mystery—and to a psychologist, such a classic approach/avoidance conflict.

Before their appointments, most presidents know very little about the role. David Riesman (1978) has written that no career line prepares for the college or university presidency. Practically, the only person who approaches the office with

---

*Power is a word that has accrued ugly connotations and makes many people uncomfortable. In this book, power refers to the human capacity to act effectively, to influence and lead other humans so as to realize a worthwhile action and its driving purpose. Power, in its purest sense, is as ethical a concept as action.

any real knowledge is someone who has previously held a successful presidency, but one presidency is usually enough for a person. For most presidents, this is the first venture into that fascinating and lonely office, a situation worlds apart from anything they have experienced before.

Many new presidents have served under other presidents, but only in lesser administrative posts. Former academic deans often find it difficult or impossible to break old patterns of behavior, even though they know that close involvement with faculty members, for example, lessens the effectiveness of their own academic dean and significantly reduces their effectiveness as president. The problem is aggravated for the faculty member who is abruptly catapulted from a professorship into the presidency with virtually no experience in management or administration. The former business executive may be better prepared for the office but find it impossible to gain the respect and appreciation of faculty members who style themselves as peers but are often reluctant to accept leadership from outsiders. The same problem exists, to a lesser degree, for a former vice president for development, public relations, business, or student services, or an assistant to a president, although previous academic appointments (preferably on another campus) are valuable preparation.

From that first day, the president is expected to perform as a master of everything—an effective combination of Abraham Lincoln, John F. Kennedy, Queen Elizabeth I, and Mother Theresa. He or she is expected to know and use effectively domains and persons heretofore foreign, from business affairs and fund raising to the care and feeding of boards of trustees and Rotary clubs. The president is expected to deal effectively with a sometimes arrogant faculty that demands results and—at the same time—demands to be equal; dissident students whose protests disregard reality; alumni who resent change and love football but expect the good reputation of Old Siwash to be maintained at all costs; demanding, demeaning, and wasteful governments; and givers who are sometimes selfish, petty, or worse. Whatever befalls the institution, the president is expected to resolve brilliantly.

Prior to their appointment, most presidents have worked in specific fields with defined tasks, where success was primarily the result of collegiality and scholarly expertise. To be suddenly thrust into a leadership role that demands additional and quite different qualities can be all but totally bewildering and at times overwhelming.

Some Presidential Missteps

Although committed and informed, perhaps it is only natural that many presidents are reluctant to be presidential. Virtually all of their pre-presidential experience is insufficient and most simply don't know enough about the nature and uses of tested power and leadership concepts and their value to an effective presidency. Not understanding how to use presidential power can create problems.

Case 1. *A college president in Massachusetts called me about a serious loyalty problem with his academic dean who, on a day of crisis for the institution, had telephoned to announce that he was taking a day's vacation. After we talked a while, the college president exploded, "Damn it, I'm going to drive right to his house and tell him what I think!" I advised him that it might be wiser to have his secretary call the dean and indicate that the president wanted to see him at a certain time, and then perhaps keep the dean cooling his heels for a while before seeing him. The president responded, "But, Jim, he lives almost an hour and a half from the campus." The president, a nice guy but dead wrong, later resigned and blamed the dean for most of his presidential problems.*

Case 2. *A dismissed state university president in New York bitterly denounced his academic vice president. "I had an uncertain feeling about the guy when I was appointed, and by my third year I knew he was working against me with the faculty. I talked to him and he assured me that I was mistaken; and, although I still had misgivings, I still couldn't bring myself to replace him. Today I know I should've fired the s.o.b." The academic vice president is still in place, and the president is looking for a job.*

Case 3. *A few years ago in Kentucky, the newly appointed president walked into the basketball arena to attend a game. He had a choice: to walk in front of the stands in full view of 15,000 fans, or to walk behind. He chose to walk behind the stands. As far as 15,000 people were concerned, the president hadn't even attended the game. He continued this kind of self-effacing behavior until he resigned three years later, declaring, "I had always thought I wanted to be a president until I became one. I just couldn't be a president."*

Case 4. *Two newly appointed presidents called in their alumni officers and summarily dismissed them. Each acted without assessing the dismissed officer's support among faculty and alumni. Although both acted within their authority, the first president resigned during his third year because of a recalcitrant constituency, and the second, after his first year in office, faced an alumni board unanimously opposed to his decision.*

Case 5. *The president of a large Middle Atlantic public university attended social functions reluctantly. Declining most invitations, she would attend no more than one each evening, usually a campus academic group. Most of her time at the event was spent engaged in serious discussion with the same people. Never considered an effective president even among those faculty members with whom she spent so much time, she simply never understood the importance of presidential presence. The same was true for the Midwestern community college president who spent $12,000 per year on faculty/staff entertainment and couldn't understand why his goals were not enthusiastically embraced by the faculty. The faculty may have liked and viewed him as a colleague, as he believed, but a faculty petition to the board indicated they certainly didn't respect him.*

Case 6. *A president of a public college in California and a small liberal arts college president in Texas couldn't understand why their faculties didn't follow their leadership. Both spent lots of time attending faculty functions and speaking on campus, taught at least one class a year, and attended departmental meetings in their disciplines. One is now teaching again and the other is barely hanging on, unwilling or afraid to maintain the distance necessary to provide the leadership the faculty wants.*

Case 7. *A president in Pennsylvania, who sat at the table as a col-*

league at campus governance meetings and stayed for the entire meeting, was perplexed because the group argued with him and didn't seem to respect his office. In his second year, the faculty already wished his more "presidential" predecessor would return.

Case 8. A college president in Pennsylvania complained of misgivings about the academic vice president's loyalty. He was confused by his lack of respect for him. "After all," he declared, "we decide everything together."

Case 9. A community-college president in Maryland had problems with faculty meetings: "I have four faculty meetings a year, and I stand right in front and encourage them to get what's bothering them off their chests." After resigning, he accepted a presidency in Texas. There are two formal faculty meetings a year; at the first, he presents a "state of the college" address, and at the second, the academic dean makes a similar address, but in more specific terms. The president enjoys Texas much more than he did Maryland.

Case 10. The president of a prestigious, private university in the South had trouble with the board and asked for a consultant to come in and speak to the trustees. "I can't understand it. I've been in office three years, and I've involved them in virtually everything that goes on. Now they give more advice than money."

There are countless other examples. There is the president who was always on time at social functions and stayed late. Another wore a polyester suit and a double windsor knot in his tie and wondered why he felt uncomfortable with local bankers and corporate heads. Another upheld merit pay for faculty until the day she was fired by the board. A fourth boasted of cleaning house the first year and was asked to resign the third. Another appointed an executive vice president his third year and had a revolution on his hands the fifth. Another, weighed down by tremendous demands on his time, didn't understand that he must get out on campus and even into the residence halls. (The story circulated about him is that "He came out of his office on February 2nd, saw his shadow, and went back in for another year.") The president who tried so hard to be friends with everyone soon returned to the faculty with his friends. Lastly, the president who refused to allocate precious resources to his public-relations, alumni, and development areas was convinced that the word would get around about the institution's excellence and that support would follow. It did, during the tenure of his successor.

Superficial indictments? Maybe somewhat. Obvious? Not to the presidents who committed these acts. Mistaken? All were, according to the research and literature on power and leadership.

Power and the Presidency

Exercising presidential power well often appears a mysterious talent, and in some respects, it is. Some presidents just seem to do it right, almost invariably coming out on top. Quite naturally, other presidents rationalize their failures by saying that the successes don't have it as tough or are just luckier, but most will usually conclude that something about the person—attitude or knowledge or style—makes things go right. When perplexed and in difficulty, troubled presidents who can screw up the courage and swallow their pride often turn to these "winners" for advice. What is this special characteristic? Why do some succeed and others fail?

A closer look at the presidency in the light of the allegory of St. Simone is in order. How does a president gain that platform and, more importantly, how can a president remain there in reasonable comfort?

How much the incumbent knows about leadership can be fundamentally valuable in the exercise of office. What the literature of power teaches can be accepted or rejected, but should at least be understood by all college or university presidents, for it reveals certain truths that can reduce the mystery of that lonely office, and can put meaning and design into what was before largely vacuous behavior. Indeed, during almost a decade as a president, the times when I seriously floundered were those when I ignored or forgot what was in the literature or when I thought I knew better. Yes, some presidents seem intuitively to grasp the basic principles of leadership, but most do not. Most seem to blunder along being a combination of what they have seen, what they think they ought to be, and what they are. All can improve their insight and performance by knowing, appreciating, and making use of the established research on leadership and power. This is not to suggest that there is only one effective presidential style, but rather that any leadership role is enhanced by an awareness of related research and experience.

Talk of leadership and power pertains to something basic to the individual psyche and to society. Virtually all psychologists, sociologists, political scientists, and even historians would agree that the ability to influence or control is one of the most important aspects of human life. Indeed, leaders are simply people who are more consistently powerful than others—everyone attempts to be influential (Katz, 1973). Surely, no thoughtful observer of human behavior would deny that human life is a ceaseless search for identity, recognition, and importance, and that this process invariably leads to attempts to influence, lead, or exert power over others. Psychologists increasingly agree that power is a central concept for any attempt to understand social behavior (Kipnis, 1976). Somehow though, people are more comfortable with the socially acceptable term, "influence," which is simply a synonym for power.

Few human expressions are not designed to influence or to impress others. This is true on the job, in politics, with friends and loved ones, in a religious or social group, or during barroom conversation. In fact, the extent to which a person successfully influences another is directly related to his or her positive self-estimate. People feel better about themselves when they convey their particular message, and become cynical and bitter if they fail. Indeed, psychoanalysts tell us that people of little power are more likely to become depressed and suffer from other mental problems. Rollo May, in *Power and Innocence*, suggests that those who are unwilling to exercise power and influence may experience unhappiness throughout their lives (May, 1972). David Kipnis suggests that virtually all studies indicate that mental health and self satisfaction are connected with position. In effect, the more resources you control, the better you feel (Kipnis, 1976). Because everyone is involved in the process of acquiring and using power, the real question boils down to the extent to which the power process is understood and used by "good" rather than "bad" persons.

Despite this, many people think of acts of power as activities engaged in by dark and pernicious figures unlike anyone they know, least of all themselves (Kipnis, 1976). Meanwhile, virtually every one of their own subtle efforts to influence another is a power act that conveys many of the same psychological consequences for them as for those dark, pernicious figures so foreign to their understanding.

Of particular interest to those involved in or aspiring to positions of leadership is the research of the highly respected psychologist, David M. McClelland, who, along with his colleague David H. Burnham, concluded that "contrary to what one might think, a good manager [or leader] is not one who needs personal success or who is people oriented, but one who likes power" (Hawker and Hall, 1981, p. 1). Quite bluntly, power is a reality of organizational (and personal) life. And the effective use of power is critical in all organizations that would possess authority and influence. McClelland and Burnham found that a strong power motivation was essential to good management; indeed, power was a more effective characteristic of effective leaders than either a need for personal achievement or a need to be liked by others. In fact, the latter two characteristics appear to act counter to effective leadership. They concluded that, "the highly self centered nature of a strong need for achievement ... leads people to behave in very special ways that do not necessarily lead to good management." The person with a strong need to be liked "is precisely the one who wants to stay on good terms with everybody and, therefore, is the one who is likely to make exceptions in terms of particular needs" (ibid., p. 1–2).

In summary, the effective leader must have a desire for impact, for being strong and influential. Moreover, this need

must be stronger than either the need for personal achievement or the need to be liked by others.

Power in Universities

In spite of these facts about power, however, the subject is
probably the most mysterious, abused, and misunderstood
human capacity (Nisbet, 1970). Although it has fascinated
man through the ages, scientists have only recently begun to
study the subject systematically; even today, there are relatively few reference citations to power (Kipnis, 1976). (This is
one reason why many observations in this book cannot be
more closely tied to related research.)

Even the literature of organization theory neglects power.
Stanford University Professor Jeffrey Pfeffer (1981) suggests
that perhaps power is too uncomfortable a subject to be com-
patible with the philosophy implied in most writing on management and leadership. In their helpful book on academic
leadership, *The Academic Administrator Grid*, Blake, Mouton, and Williams (1981) do not even discuss the subject; and,
in almost 350 bibliographic citations, they list fewer than a
dozen authors who have published significantly in the field.
And, as is the case with many observers of tranquil times, they
seem more concerned with harmony than with results. While
harmonious relationships in organizations, of course, are
good, they do not necessarily spring from egalitarianism.

Because ideology and practice often conflict, it is understandable, if not theoretically sound, to ignore topics—such as
power—that detract from the fundamental theory served by
the writing. At American colleges and universities, although
power is understood, few will discuss the subject candidly
because it violates normative and comfortable beliefs about
the nature of universities and academic life. A study at the
University of Illinois, based on interviews with twenty-nine
department heads, asked each respondent to rate the power of
all the university departments; only one department head
needed to ask for clarification of the term "power" (Pfeffer,

1981). There was "enormous" consistency in the ratings, particularly of the most and least powerful departments. Many perceive the very asking of these questions as illegitimate and upsetting. During a study at two University of California campuses conducted by Pfeffer (1981), one humanities department chairperson, after reviewing a copy of the questionnaire in advance of the interview, refused to cooperate with the study: "If I saw the university in the terms implied in your questionnaire, I would be seeking, frankly, some other way of making a living, instead of practicing the profession I've been engaged in for the last three decades."

Yet, interest in power seems normal and even popular. In book stores one often notices at least two anxious coveys of people each looking furtively over his or her shoulder to see if anyone is watching. They are huddled around the books on sex and pornography—how to be more attractive, lovable, and sexy—and the books on power and influence—how to be more important, assertive, and successful. This was dramatized recently as Michael Korda's *Power: How to Get It, How to Use It* (1976) became the nation's number one bestseller. Korda's book told us where to sit, what to wear, and what kind of briefcase to carry; although not well-documented, it wasn't far off the mark.

And power is a subject about which leaders—perhaps especially college presidents in this case—are seldom candid. The current style has been to apologize for using the authority of position and to speak of its terrible burdens. The secret seems to be to contrive a pose of refined disinterest and modesty behind which one wields all the power possible. Unfortunately, or perhaps fortunately, it doesn't work this way, as the departure from office of one U.S. president demonstrated.

During recent years, I have spoken on this subject to several groups of college presidents and academic deans, numbering in the several hundreds. Presidents are always attentive, though often uncomfortable and silent, and the academic deans are sometimes downright hostile. But many later want to speak in private about the subject—even the deans! And, as of this writing, they continue to write and call.

There are those who hold that administration (leadership) is more of an art than a science, and there is certainly much to support this position. Nonetheless, the larger measure of this book is the result of having attempted to apply the results of research in the fields of leadership and power for almost ten years in a college presidency. This is not to suggest that research will always show a clear and certain path, but it can influence the course of action. And, in the least, knowledge of studies in these fields can provide confirming reassurance to the president who always behaved that way in the first place.

After attempting to establish further the need for strong presidential leadership, the research and discussion presented in the forthcoming chapters establishes that understanding tested techniques of leadership and power can contribute significantly to the strength and progress of any institution —company, country, or college.* If the mission is worth pursuing, so is this kind of knowledge. Of course, although examples of the use of power are presented, how presidential power is employed remains a personal matter that can be determined only by an incumbent president. The key is to make the most of it.

   ★ Enjoy the presidency.

   ★ Relax; after you're gone a year, well, maybe two, you won't even be missed.

   ★ You are the president, whether it fits comfortably or not.

   ★ Never, never get off that presidential platform

   ★ Never act beneath your office, but don't hide behind it either.

---

*The reader should bear in mind that, in the chapters discussing the use of power by a college president (Chapters 4 through 13), the research is only loosely related to the presentation; but the knowledge of research did inspire both the presidential prescription and much of my own presidential behavior.

* Stand when you speak; if you do it right, only you will know your feet are in sand.

* At least once a week, show up where you are least expected.

* Try not to mix personal life and business.

CHAPTER 2

Leadership

*The strongest is never strong enough to always be the master
unless he transforms strength into right and obedience into duty.*

Jean Jacques Rousseau

*Leadership is the art of getting someone else to do something you
want done because he wants to do it.*

Dwight D. Eisenhower

Yes, but it helps if you're tall and good looking.

Lou Costello

OF ALL THE PROBLEMS confronting higher education in the coming years, the greatest will be leadership, according to Clark Kerr (1980). A recent Carnegie Report concluded that in the face of the pressures of governments, unions, and corporations, the rebirth of strong leadership "may well be the central question facing American higher education." David Riesman (1978) has written that, "increasingly, the American college presidency appears to be faceless." Frederick W. Ness of the Association of American Colleges Presidential Search Office has commented that, "most trustees seem more interested in plant managers and technicians as presidents than leaders" (Ness, 1980; personal interview). Joseph Kauffman, in his excellent book, *At the Pleasure of the Board* (1980), writes of the problems of democratization, centralized systems, and collective bargaining and their debilitating effects on the presidency. Richard Cyert concluded after an analysis of the problems facing higher education that all institutions—whether public or private, large or small, rich or poor, coeducational or

15

single sex—will require strong presidents who can lead and act (1980). And Fred M. Hechinger in the *New York Times* concluded that "the most successful college presidents, even in attracting financial support, are those who are not afraid to make waves."

The Strong Presidency

Leadership will be a greater problem during the 1980s than inflation, increasing expenses, declining government support, curriculum rebuilding, or declining enrollments. Yet a member of a presidential selection committee at a distinguished Midwestern university said, "I can't tell you who we're going to appoint, but I'm sure it will be the wrong person." But most do not write of presidents as strong leaders. Presidents are described as "mediators," "support mechanisms," "chairs," "managers of human resources," "apostles of efficiency," "energy maximizers," "reasonable adventurers," "catalysts of dynamic contacts," or even "sweepers and dusters" (Pray, 1979; Walker, 1979; Chickering, 1981; Mayhew and Glenny, 1975; Hodgkinson, 1970; Cohen and March, 1974; Editorial Projects for Education, 1976). As early as 1959, Harold Stoke speculated as to why anyone would want to be a college president and stated that a successful president could not enjoy the office (Stoke, 1959). Most recently, Stephen K. Bailey called American college presidents a "beleaguered lot," citing Charles Eliot's reminder that the prime requisite of presidential success is a "willingness to give pain" (Argyris and Cyert, 1980). A former president expressed it this way: "The president seldom has time to take stock of how well or how badly he is doing until he bails out or runs screaming for the horizon or achieves the inner peace of complete breakdown" (Carbone, 1981).

If we consider conditions on the campus during recent years, many of these observations are thoughtful and logical, but to some they are rationalizations for poor presidential leadership. In effect, observers are telling presidents that conditions simply aren't appropriate for good leadership—that students, faculty, trustees, politicians, and the public will no longer support strong leadership—thus giving presidents, particularly newly appointed ones, a respectable excuse for being less effective. When writers conclude it unlikely that current leadership and management conditions in higher education will change, the result is bound to be a self-fulfilling prophecy. Yet, in spite of the current insistence of virtually all segments of the college community to be more involved (Chickering, 1981), faculty members today dislike the "nice guy" president who professes to make all the decisions democratically as much as they dislike the "devious president"; and students as well as faculty "know" that the president has final say in most matters (Benezet et al., 1981).

There are even those whose view of leadership assumes that, unless a president takes risks, he or she is unworthy of the faith and support of those who granted the unique power and responsibility of the presidency. Most of these inspired statements refer to presidents in the corporate and business sector (Henschel, 1971). With growing appreciation, I recall what my mentor, Dr. Robert G. Bone, told me while I was serving as his assistant: "Jim, the college president who doesn't feel inside that he may be putting his job on the line at least once each year is either unworthy of the office or times are so tranquil that the office is unworthy of him." Also reassuring is research in the field of leadership, which identified "boldness" as a requisite for effective leadership as long as forty years ago (Bird, 1940), and as recently as 1981 (Pfeffer).

Without towering presidents, men and women of ability and courage, the problems of the immediate future will become more serious. Many agree that the very nature, and perhaps even the very existence, of some worthy institutions are at stake. Dramatic reductions in support, stifling constraints on both public and independent colleges and universities by state agencies, federal controls, more powerful faculty and student groups, and anxious boards of trustees promise a future that will be anything but easy. At a recent Harvard Symposium on Leadership, the participants concluded that if higher education doesn't produce "crusader" presidents in the 1980s, they will come from some other sector of society (Maerhoff in Argyris and Cyert, 1980). Strong presidents will be most successful in the coming decades, and they will be called on both to defend their institutions and to inspire their people.

Some Historic Reminders about Leadership

Leadership ability is not an innate characteristic of only the privileged few; people are not born with it. Leadership subsumes certain measurable characteristics that can be cultivated by virtually all college or university presidents.

Although the word "leadership" was first coined in the early 1800s, people possessing its characteristics have lived throughout human history. History is written around these people. The Reformation is the story of Luther, Calvin, and Zwingli; the French Revolution, of Voltaire, Robespierre, Danton, and Marat; and the Russian Revolution, of Lenin, Trotsky, and Stalin. So it is with higher education; institutions have been personified by the presidents who presided over them: Eliot of Harvard, Harper of Chicago, Jordan of Stanford, White of Cornell, Hutchins of Chicago, Wells of Indiana, Angell of Michigan, Hanna of Michigan State, Hesburgh of Notre Dame, Kerr of California, Dumke of California, and Brewster of Yale. Jordan was selected as the first president of Stanford because he was a "firm-minded" executive and could "manage things like a railroad" (Veysey, 1965). There are countless regional examples of strong presidents who have brought vitality and distinction to their institutions. And recent studies indicate that in spite of the egalitarianism of the recent past in American higher education, perceptive analysts who study college campuses can quickly discern the nature of leadership of an institution by observing the accomplishments and sensing the ambiance of the place (Benezet et al., 1981). Yet, as higher education today faces difficulties greater than any in recent history, there are few bold or strong leaders.

Leadership in Higher Education Today

Many observers of higher education today cite only two American university presidents who transcend their institutions in terms of broad influence and stature. They are Father Theodore Hesburgh of Notre Dame and the very controversial John Silber of Boston University. Some are beginning to add Steven Muller of Johns Hopkins to the list.

The young Hesburgh exceeded the expectations of the Order of the Holy Cross that appointed him; he upset many religious leaders in Catholic higher education, and he is sometimes credited as the person who made Catholic higher education respectable (MacEoin, 1976). Silber brought a struggling Boston University out of the red, helped to recruit a generally excellent faculty, and made the name of the university a household word. When he has problems with the faculty, he is invited to discuss the situation on the country's most popular television news show, "60 Minutes." Muller boldly but sensitively engaged a strong and traditional faculty, brought a distinguished but wandering medical school under control, and raised more private support for the university than all of his predecessors put together had done. He also challenged the federal government as a pernicious influence and led a movement to create a new national association to combat excessive government intervention in higher education. (Today, that association, the National Association of Independent Colleges and Universities, is one of the most significant forces in Washington.)

Many believe that these kinds of presidents would not be hired by most boards of trustees today. All are leaders. And although they are each quite different in many respects, they apparently believe that college presidents should be visible and at times controversial and that higher education is too important to be left to popular drift, to autonomous faculty and student committees, to government constraints, or to caretaker presidents.

Studies appear to support the styles of these presidents. Contrary to beliefs espoused by many involved in recent

movements in higher education and society in general, directive leadership has been found to be more effective than nondirective (Burke, 1966; Thiagarajan and Deep, 1970; McClelland, 1969, 1975; McClelland and Burnham, 1976; Steers, 1981). People seem to want an astute, strong, assertive figure who involves them in the decision-making process but makes the final decision and accepts responsibility for it. This runs counter to the popular centralist notion regarding leadership in higher education. Nonetheless, if it works for you, use it, but consider with some reservation the advisor who has never held a presidency (scholar or not) or the president who has never been in combat.

Research on Leadership

Leaders who operate less extensively throughout their organization and who retain final authority are more likely to be accurately perceived and to realize desired organizational structure and goals (Scott, 1956; McClelland, 1975). Clearly, one purpose of leadership roles is to maintain institutional stability and responsiveness. Other studies suggest that group members do not develop or accept group norms and expectations unless these are well defined by those in leadership positions, and that too much informal or familiar behavior on the part of leaders tends to reduce their perceived legitimacy (Clark, 1956; McClelland, 1975; Pfeffer, 1981). The overly folksy presidents discussed in Chapter 1 may soon become one of the folks again. The ideal combination is familiarity but always from the presidential platform. Don't pretend to be what you are not: you are the president.

There is also evidence that norms or policies tend to be better accepted the longer they are in force, and that leaders under such circumstances tend to be more readily accepted (Torrance, 1954; French and Raven, 1968). People seem inclined to accept conditions simply because, "That's the way it's always been"; thus, the value of citing precedent.

Research also indicates that an appointment rather than

election to a position makes a leader more effective (Julian, Hollander, and Regula, 1969). Indeed, although elections make the leader more immediately likable, in the long run the elected leader is less secure and more vulnerable to censure. After experiencing early success, appointed leaders are more likely to be admired by their followers.

This raises many questions about the impact of the democratization movement in higher education that took place from 1963 to 1978. For example, does the increasingly broad representation on presidential selection committees—everyone from students to administrative and nonacademic staff—tend to dilute the perceived legitimacy of the governing board? Implicitly at least, does this subject the president to the whim and caprice of the academic community and prevent him or her from providing the leadership that the community needs and expects?

Research suggests that members of a community expect their leaders to try to influence them (Torrance, 1959; Benezet et al., 1981). A leader who simply tries to reflect the wishes of the constituency or who declares neutrality on many key issues may be abrogating responsibility and is often destined for a short term. This is especially true during conditions of difficulty. Disruptive behavior, antagonism, tension, and absenteeism increase under poorly defined and nondirective situations (Burke, 1966). People, including educated people, want and need structure, and an informed leader knows that if a majority opposition coalition develops, it not only may undermine presidential effectiveness but the coalition itself may informally assume the leadership position (Caplow, 1968).* On a campus, the key is for the president to provide structured opportunities for participation by faculty, students, and staff, but clearly to retain final authority and responsibility; for,

---

*A number of articles and books have been written during recent years about the various Japanese management and production systems, which are largely egalitarian and familial in nature. Indeed, not only have some American companies established plants in Japan, others have incorporated Japanese techniques in plants located in the United States and using largely U.S.

indeed, this is what faculty and students expect from their president (Benezet et al., 1981).

Early studies concluded that leadership involved certain personal characteristics but that it was also situational; that is, different skills or qualities amount to leadership in different situations (Bird, 1940; Jenkins, 1947; Stogdill, 1948). Studies conducted before 1940 correlate only four of seventy-nine traits with leadership in general: a sense of humor, above-average intelligence, extroversion, and boldness or willingness to take the initiative (Bird, 1940). Twenty years later, other characteristics were added to the list: courage, fortitude (persistence), and sensitivity (Mann, 1959). And throughout the period of systematic studies of leadership, leaders were found to be male, white, and generally attractive.

A decade later, it was found that years of experience in one leadership role were not apparently related to the effectiveness of leadership as measured by productivity (Fiedler, 1970). There appears to be a point of diminishing returns for most leaders—a point in time beyond which they lose effectiveness. College presidents should know that there are really very few Father Hesburghs. By the 1970s, it was found that physical characteristics were not as important as earlier studies had reported. The democratization movement of the period obviously affected the popular image of leaders. While being a tall, attractive, white man is not necessarily a disadvantage in achieving leadership, these characteristics no longer seem to give one an automatic edge.

More recent research suggests that leaders have or appear to have inordinate reserves of energy and stamina, and to maintain unusually good physical condition. Even those handicapped by physical disability or poor health tend to display great vigor (Stogdill, 1974). The effective leader always appears

---

workers. These models will not be discussed here. The writer views the early success of these systems in Japan as being relatively untested and, therefore, significantly influenced by the halo effect, and that both uncertain efficiency and cultural differences make the adoption of these techniques in the United States questionable.

to have energy left over. And the leader's personal characteristics and values must appear to fit the needs and aspirations of his or her following (Katz, 1973).

Socioeconomic background was once believed to play a significant role in creating leaders (Mathews, 1954). While "good family" is not a disadvantage, recent studies report proportionately more top executives from poorer and middle-income backgrounds than from the wealthier upper classes (*Scientific American*, 1965). Religious and ethnic background apparently remain significant factors in upward mobility within formal organizations, but recent studies contrasting effective with adequate college presidents conclude that social background, race, and religion were of little importance (Pruitt, 1974). Effective presidents were generally younger (early forties rather than early fifties), had taught fewer years (fewer than five rather than more than ten), had a stronger sense of mission, and were not necessarily educated in a traditional academic discipline. Women executives, once in middle management, find it more difficult than men to rise further (Cussler, 1958). But educational level does tend to offset disadvantageous socioeconomic, gender, or racial factors.

The relationship of intelligence to leadership is interesting. Early studies found that leaders much brighter than their followers were less successful (Stogdill, 1948). Later studies found that leaders whose intelligence was consistent with their followers' were more successful than leaders whose intelligence scores were either low or very high (Ghiselli, 1963). Intelligence, as measured by verbal-ability tests, appears to be related to first-level supervisory performance but the higher in the management hierarchy, the less significant this correlation. Intelligence does not appear to be a real predictor of success at these levels (Korman, 1968). Indeed, a survey of managers to identify effective political actors ranked high intelligence and logic the last two of thirteen related characteristics (Allen et al., 1979). There is evidence, however, that leaders do tend to have superior judgment, decisiveness, knowledge, and fluency of speech (Stogdill, 1974).

Although the elements of chance and timing probably play

a part in the rise of individuals, the newly appointed college president should know that today effective leaders are generally characterized by such qualities as: a strong drive for responsibility, vigor, persistence, willingness to take chances, originality, ability to delegate, humor, initiative in social situations, fairness, self-confidence, decisiveness, sense of identity, personal style, capacity to organize, willingness to act or boldness, willingness to share the credit for successes and absorb virtually all of the stress of failure, and tolerance of frustration and delay (a quality undoubtedly induced by the advent of bureaucracies). All of these together constitute an ability to influence the behavior of others.

Presidential leadership, then, will be of vital importance during the immediate future of higher education and, according to many observers, strong leadership is in short supply in the college presidency today. The reasons may have more to do with the recent democratization period in our society and on our campuses than with the current incumbents who often find themselves severely limited by the internal constraints of powerful faculty, student, and even administrative groups and the external constraints imposed by overinvolved and highly socialized governing boards and, in the public sector, by increasingly strong state systems (Fisher, 1980).*

Nonetheless, strong leadership is an imperative of the future and will probably be facilitated by the converging difficulties (inflation, enrollment reduction, and declining government support) that will force a return to stronger leadership.

The following chapter on power and the presidency reviews the most significant research on this always intriguing

---

*As of this writing, there is no evidence, to my knowledge, that state systems have either brought increased efficiency or improved programs to higher education; rather, the contrary is the case. Since the advent of state systems, costs have gone up and the general achievement levels of college graduates have gone down. The only argument for state systems is that costs might have gone up and educational quality gone down faster without them. This argument is specious.

and sometimes unsettling subject, and attempts to enable the reader to establish a tentative design for presidential leadership.

* The college or university that isn't going forward is going backward.

* Don't be too impressed with Harvard.

* If anyone ever calls you unctuous, examine your motives and buy a sports car.

* Make as many changes and debatable decisions as possible during your honeymoon in office. It will establish a design for change, create precedent, and be accepted by the community. Don't listen seriously to the person who says, "Wait till you get the feel of the place." It's too late then.

* To accomplish goals, use anything within the limits of ethics and a reasonable propriety, including cajolery, flattery, and persuasion.

* There is an aura of victory that surrounds a person of good will.

* Cultivate the people and keep the common touch.

* Travel.

CHAPTER 3

Power

The problem of power is how to achieve its responsible use rather than its irresponsible and indulgent use—of how to get men of power to live for the public rather than off the public.

Robert Kennedy

Life is a search after power; this is an element with which the earth is saturated.

Ralph Waldo Emerson

I repeat . . . that all power is a trust; that we are accountable for its exercise; that, from the people, and for the people, all springs, and all must exist.

Benjamin Disraeli

WHY CAN A SINGLE PERSON influence others, even exercise control over a large group? How does one explain the influence of a John F. Kennedy, Dwight D. Eisenhower, Winston Churchill, Lenin, Socrates, Jesus, Cleopatra, Queen Victoria, Mao Tse-tung, Catherine the Great, Abraham Lincoln, or George Washington? Or in the contemporary American college presidency of Father Theodore Hesburgh, Steven Muller, Derek Bok, Kingman Brewster, Terry Sanford, Peter Magrath, James Scales, Stephen Trachtenberg, Father Joseph Sellinger, Hanna Gray, Father Timothy Healy, William Friday, William Banowsky, Charles Odegaard, William Tolley, Henry Wriston, Bartlett Giamatti, John Toll, John Silber, and others including a growing number of presidents who lead small liberal arts colleges and regional two- and four-year institutions.

For our purposes, power is the answer, but what is power? Is it birthright? A natural characteristic? Being in the right place at the right time? Being at Harvard? Is it something one learns? Can anyone gain power? How can it be most ethically exercised?

Until 1960, there were fewer than forty published studies on power, many of them comprised entirely of the subjective opinions of the authors. Since then, researchers have used techniques of better quality and conducted more than 250 studies, many of which are cited in this chapter.

There are many definitions of power. It has been defined as, "the probability that one actor within a social relationship will be in a position to carry out his own will despite resistance, regardless of the basis on which this probability rests" (Weber, 1947); as "the ability to employ force" (Bierstedt, 1950); and "the ability of A to get B to do something that B would otherwise not do" (Dahl, 1957); or, as kings have known, the ability to get people to wait for you and to be thrilled when you arrive.

Most researchers agree that the bases of power are diverse, varying from one situation to another, and that people or a combination of conscious and unconscious factors are utilized in the attempt to influence others. For purposes of analysis, convenience, and discussion, these characteristics are elaborated in a topology (French and Raven, 1959) since used by other researchers and adopted for this book: coercive power, reward power, legitimate power, expert power, and referent or charismatic power. In other words, all attempts to influence other researchers and adopted for this book: *coercive power, reward power, legitimate power, expert power, and referent or charismatic power.* In other words, all attempts to influence employ a combination of these power forms, and the intention of this chapter is to present much of the most significant research on the subject of power in a way that can be especially useful for college presidents.

Before discussing the forms of power, however, it is important to distinguish between one's motives for power (although any power motive, base or altruistic, yields results). According to McClelland (1969, 1975), one's desire for impact, strength, or influence may take either of two forms: (1) it may be oriented primarily toward the achievement of personal gain and aggrandizement, or (2) it may be motivated by the need to influence others' behavior for the common good. In the first instance, the need for power is essentially self-serving and is very likely colored by unresolved achievement needs. In the second instance, the person's power motivation is often labeled "socialized" (as opposed to "personalized"), and power is valued as an instrument to be used for the common good on behalf of the whole organization and its members. Either power motivation, however, better equips a person to lead than does a purely achievement or affiliative orientation. Today there are even standardized tests available to determine one's level and kind of power motivation (Hall and Hawker, 1981). The thesis of this book is that college and university presidents' power motivation is "socialized" (for the common good). The reader will please bear this in mind. Motivation is important also in that it determines the type of follower attracted.

Coercive Power

Coercive power employs threats and punishments to gain compliance and is the least effective kind of power for a college president. Studies indicate that the threat of punishment induces greater conformity than punishment itself (Raven and French, 1957). More recently, researchers have discovered that the leader's perceived legitimacy reduces resistance to conformity and makes punishment more acceptable to the punished. If a leader is generally admired, followers more readily accept the implied use of penalties, but once punishment is actually used, the leader becomes less effective (French, Morrison, and Levinger, 1960; Iverson, 1964). People will work harder for a leader they find attractive (charismatic) and legitimate than for one who is perceived as coercive (Zander and Curtis, 1962). Nonetheless, the threat of punishment does tend to induce compliance and can serve as a deterrence to hostile behavior so long as the punishments are respected and feared (Kipnis, 1976).

We have also learned that maturity tends to reduce the already questionable value of punishment as a motivating condition; that, indeed, more mature groups tend to be more productive under less punitive conditions (Kipnis and Wagner, 1967). However, even highly educated people are willing to administer punishment when commanded to do so by established authority figures. The Milgram studies established this to a rather frightening extent (Milgram, 1965). When individuals were ordered to administer "dangerous" degrees of electric shock to others, they almost invariably did so. They became less inclined to obey such instructions only when they were permitted to observe those who refused to do so. We also have reason to believe that when persons are allowed to react more extensively with peers in the group, they are less inclined to identify with coercive leaders (Stotland, 1959). There is also evidence that suggests that less confident leaders tend to rely more heavily on coercive and legitimate power than on other forms of influence (Kipnis, 1976).

It is well established that when other forms of power are wanting—that is, when a supervisor, or a college president, is not granted sufficient authority to exercise power (by a board of trustees or a faculty)—he or she may be more inclined to use covert and coercive means to obtain ends (Tedeschi, Schlenker, and Bonoma, 1973; Jones, 1964; Kipnis and Venderveer, 1971). Therefore, presidents who have either allowed their power to be assumed by faculty, students, and staff or have been stripped of power by governing boards will be less effective because they do not have the ability (power) to grant the privilege of participation; it is simply assumed as a right by the participants. These same presidents are also bound to develop lower feelings of self-worth and reduced expectations of successful influence, which in turn leads to a greater reliance upon the use of coercion. Under these conditions, virtually all leaders are moved to use fear, arousal, and stealth as influence techniques (Kipnis, 1976). Clearly, as the powerholder's expectations of successful influence are lowered, there is an increasing tendency to exert more pressure by the use of coercive influence (Goodstadt and Hjelle, 1973).

Raven, one of the principal researchers in the field, concludes that if the "goal of the powerholder is to produce long-lasting changes in behavior, then the powerholder would probably avoid coercive means of influence" (1974). However, if long-lasting compliance is not an issue, then the powerholder might decide to invoke stronger, more coercive sanctions.

In summary, although the threat of punishment or penalty tends to induce compliance, an astute leader uses it seldom, if ever. On those rare occasions, the research suggests that the individual punished should be isolated as much as possible from support in the community. Making a public example of someone, however, may prove useful, since the action will not remain secret long anyway. Never apply punishment in anger or pique but only after thoughtful deliberation, which will usually suggest another, wiser, and more just form of disapproval that better serves your worthy goals.

Reward Power

Reward power implies the ability of one individual to accomplish desired outcomes by favors, recognition, or rewards to group members. Studies have revealed some noteworthy and slightly disconcerting observations. For example, high-status persons—like college and university presidents—tend to compromise the stated goals of their organization or group more readily than others: the higher the office, the more likely the leader is to compromise (Mills, 1953). Authority figures who yield too readily to their group are more likely to be exploited by it (Swingle, 1970). This augurs well for the leader's maintaining some psychological distance from the members of the group, which will be discussed later in this chapter. Nice guys, at least to the degree that they compromise their office, do finish last.

Although difficult to do, it is often better to reward those we do not like or those we feel dissimilar to than those to whom we are attracted (Tedeschi, Schlenker, and Bonoma,

1973; Baker, DiMarco, and Scott, 1975; Banks, 1974). This statement assumes that it is easier to influence those who are attractive or similar to us, and that more effort is required with others. The main message is that the effective leader rewards those who support the goals of the organization, regardless of personal feeling. Rewards are also a way to bring personality opposites into the fold. Unfortunately, rewards too often are employed to prevent rather than to eliminate existing resistance (Lawler, 1971). Anyone who relies heavily on reward power should reward contributing supporters, but potential converts should also be given positive attention.

Rewards are not likely to change attitudes permanently. Rather, as soon as rewards cease, it is highly probable that the person will revert to original attitudes and behavior (Raven and Kruglanski, 1970). Furthermore, a focus of resentment results from withholding the rewards. The lesson is not to expect too much from bestowing recognition, favors, or money on members of your organization. This fact argues strongly for the use of expert and charismatic power, discussed later.

Other observations support the position that reward power is a weak instrument for change (Foa and Foa, 1975). It is easy to assume that money is an effective way to insure support, admiration, or affection, but this thinking is not attuned to human psychology; love can't be bought. Machiavelli warned the Prince that "liberality" (rewards) could not guarantee that the Prince would be held in high regard by his followers (Machiavelli, 1952). Machiavelli even concluded that it was better to be feared than to try to gain support with rewards.

In relatively democratic situations, like college and university campuses, coalitions almost invariably develop and parity emerges as a social principle (Thibaut and Gruder, 1969). Left without structure, contractual agreements develop and power is diffused. Participants develop feelings of identification between each other, resulting in parity without discrimination and a reduction in the effectiveness of the leader (Murdoch, 1967). During the late 1960s and the 1970s, the concept of "equality" over "equity" gained even more acceptance. More and more people found "share and share alike" to be more acceptable than the traditional notion that rewards followed upon personal effort (Lenner, 1974).

Reward power works for the leader, but in a highly democratic society, its use requires exceptional care. Most persons in reward-yielding situations develop feelings of responsibility for one another, thus the development of informal and subtle contractual agreements that result in greater acceptance of parity and equity, rather than a sharply differentiating system of reward distribution. This kind of situation can bode difficulty for a college president as he or she attempts to reconcile the conflicting demands of merit pay and popular position.

A university president, while reserving final salary authority over the administration, should probably delegate responsibility for faculty salary and promotion to academic administrators who work with elected faculty committees, in an effort to direct the controversy elsewhere, as there will always be controversy in salary matters. Of course, the president should retain final authority and review all salaries, but should rarely exercise this authority with faculty members. (In the case of collective bargaining, reward power is so diffused that it is virtually nonexistent.)

Except for key administrative associates, the most effective use of reward power for the college president is usually more subtle and nebulous than tangible awards; for example, selective words, notes of praise, and appointments to administrative and key committee posts. There is no substitute for thoughtful, deliberate, emotional acknowledgment and support from the president. Positive equivocation regarding the specifics of academic promotion and salaries is wisest. Presidents should bear in mind that there are limits to the secure and effective use of reward power.

Legitimate Power

Legitimate power is based on a group's acceptance of common beliefs and practices. The acceptance of these practices and values, which include the distribution of influence within the particular social setting, binds those members together through their common perspective. The group adheres to leaders who appear to fit certain roles consistent with their expectations, endowing those persons who assume leadership with certain power. Certain activities and actions come to be expected and accepted from those leaders and are considered legitimate within that context. Some consider this condition as authority rather than power (Pfeffer, 1981), while others style it as another form of power. For our purposes, the simpler version will do—that is, the acceptance of common norms enables a leader to exercise power that otherwise might not be accepted by the group. By so legitimizing power, its exercise is transformed in a remarkable way, for it makes the use of all other power forms (coercive, reward, expert, and charismatic) more acceptable to the group. For instance, in most social situations, the exercise of power involves costs. There is an expenditure of resources, the making of commitments, a greater need to rely on the other power forms and, in effect, use up one's potential for influencing the group. Clearly, the possession of legitimate power or authority will, if used effectively, significantly enhance the effectiveness of the leader. Indeed, persons in legitimate authority positions are expected to use their authority, and at times are even punished for not doing so (Dornbusch and Scott, 1975).

A common and troublesome situation arises when a delegated leader will not discharge his or her office. I term this a "power vacuum," the antithesis of a competent application of power leadership. This occurs when the appointed leader, for whatever reason, will not assume the responsibilities of the office. Assignment to a leadership role does not confer any leadership abilities. Unfortunately, an individual may be promoted to a position of authority and, by inaction, create a torpor and inertia around himself or herself. The power is then assumed by coworkers or subordinates and is diffused and diminished until some adjustment is effected.

Three bases of legitimate power are generally recognized: (1) cultural values that endow some group members with the right to exercise power; (2) occupancy of a position recognized to confer authority; and (3) appointment or designation as a leader by a legitimizing agent. "In all cases, the notion of legitimacy involves some sort of code or standard accepted by the individual, by virtue of which the external agent can exercise his power" (French and Raven, 1959). Legitimate power is exercised by persons who hold titles that imply authority—father, mother, judge, president, doctor, police officer, captain, director, senator, or dean.

Contrary to what many of us thought as young faculty members—"If I could run this university for a day, I'd show them how to get something done"—studies show that people generally follow legitimate leaders with whom they agree. Those with whom they disagree are likely to be sent packing or ignored to the extent possible. While legitimate power is a significant element of influence and control, it is not as effective as most people think. People who do not at least reluctantly agree will often disobey or ignore their employers, political leaders, and other authority figures and, in extreme cases, even try to do them in. Legitimate leaders who noticeably overstep the bounds of their roles invite needless resistance.

Nonetheless, it is important to emphasize that within formal organizations such as colleges and universities, norms and expectations invariably develop that make the exercise of power expected and accepted. Thus, social control of one's behavior becomes an expected part of college or university life. And legitimate power is of fundamental importance to a college president, for, rather than becoming a contest of strength or contesting wills, once power is transformed through legitimization, it is not resisted unless it is abused or ineffectively used. At the point of legitimization, it no longer depends on the resources or arguments or power that produced it in the first place, for it can stand alone as a form of power. Indeed, the more legitimate the leader becomes, the more the leader is accepted by the group (Clark, 1956). And, the more legitimate the leader, the more effectively he or she can exercise the "incremental" forms of power that follow —expert and charismatic power.

Legitimate power is maintained, then, not so much by its originating sanctions, but rather by the degree to which the group continues to adhere to the common and unifying bonds that produced the legitimate leader in the first place. If a holder of legitimate power, such as a parent, a corporate officer, a judge, or a college president, conducts the office poorly, then power again becomes diffused, and the group spends more time in conflict than in growth. As has been suggested, legitimate power adds stability to the group and can only be used effectively after one thoroughly understands and appreciates the other forms of power.

It is also fairly well established that group members perceive the organization's status structure more accurately when high-status members react less extensively throughout the organization and retain final authority in their own hands. Indeed, legitimate power is largely dependent on the extent to which group members perceive the role in the first place (Scott, 1956). Indeed, people are less inclined toward resentment and hostility when they are operating under common and understood norms and with fully legitimized leaders (Cohen, 1953). Furthermore, appointed leaders are generally considered more legitimate and effective than elected leaders. (Julian, Hollander, and Rejuda, 1969). Election, rather than making a leader more secure and effective, tends to result in anxiety, insecurity, and vulnerability.

One further word here: the recent documentation of the loss of public confidence in most contemporary institutions, including higher education, has consequences for decision making and governance of colleges and universities. The acceptance of some form of authority is critical to all forms of organizations (Mechanic, 1962). It is impossible to exercise control of general direction through the use of rewards and punishments, nor can it be done with any measure of efficiency through the exclusive use of expert or charismatic power. Legitimate power allows one to make choices in a fashion that approximates the rational model (Pfeffer, 1981). To the extent that authority is eroded through the loss of confidence and legitimacy, participants are less likely to accept decisions without question. What was once a rational process for decision making becomes a political struggle that can be the very undoing of the institution itself. And it takes a masterful, legitimate leader to overcome the currents of the general society effectively.

In sum, legitimate power is an effective and necessary form of presidential power, and people tend to be more accepting of a legitimate leader when they are in fundamental agreement with his or her policies and actions. The legitimate leader will be effective to the extent that he or she appreciates and uses the various other forms of power. Most reasonably intelligent and educated people can be effective legitimate leaders. Although election to a leadership role is preferable to emergence through group interaction, being appointed seems to be the best way of all to insure effectiveness. Leaders who present themselves as being legitimate tend, in fact, to be more powerful. They are generally better liked and their influence attempts are more accepted.

Expert and charismatic power, which follow, represent a kind of "incremental power" characteristic of an individual, while legitimate, reward, and coercive power tend to be organizationally derived (Student, 1968). Most persons of reasonable ability and motivation can exercise these last three forms of power, but those who adroitly use charismatic and expert power can be and usually are the most effective leaders.

Expert Power

Expert power, which reflects the deference accorded a perceived authority, tends to legitimize leaders and make them more effective. Expert power, in most circumstances, is the most consistently effective kind of power among those discussed so far in this chapter (Luchins and Luchins, 1961), particularly for college and university presidents. There are two ways of wielding the influence of an expert. By being introduced to a group as an expert, unless you commit a monumental blunder, you will be the controlling influence in the group. Or, you can actually become an expert, a person who is knowledgeable and informed about the subject at hand (Zander, 1953; Zander and Cohen, 1955; Mausner, 1953).

For instance, Lowe and Shaw (1968, in Pfeffer, 1981) found that even though attempts to project future conditions were suspected of being inaccurate, such forecasts were accepted and influential in decision making. It is also true that the withholding of information or expertise is a measurably significant power form (Pettigrew, 1972, in Pfeffer, 1981).

Clearly, as a leader attempts to garner support for a particular cause, it is valuable for him or her to be perceived as an expert, for it both inspires support for a common cause and reduces unproductive conflict. The important thing is that the leader be a true authority on both the nature and condition of the enterprise. The acceptance of such forecasting occurs because of the time and effort it takes for an opponent to gather information for an alternative position as well as the implied lack of trust and confidence that such a course suggests; and most are not willing to risk the loss of popularity that is at stake when going against the leader.

Research further demonstrates the value of perceived expertise: People being introduced as prestigious feel better accepted and more at ease than people being assigned low-prestige roles, and they are measurably more effective and influential (Zander and Cohen, 1955). One would think that people introducing guest speakers would one day get this message. Your own introduction as a president, both on and off campus, is important here, unless you are a former Secretary of State.

Groups with more than one expert are apparently less certain of their judgment, and the experts are less effective (Torrance and Aliotti, 1965; Collaros and Anderson, 1969). This perhaps explains the old military adage, "It's better to have one idiot in charge than two geniuses." Indeed, the more acknowledged experts in a group or community, the less effective their expert powers; even the experts become inhibited. Or, as college presidents could title this observed fact, "The trouble with unstructured faculty meetings." Indeed, studies have found that, in groups with many experts, high status rather than expertise can be the more significant determinant of behavior (Torrance, 1955). Combining expertise with high position is the most effective posture in virtually any situation, provided that expertise is consistently shown. It follows that college and university presidents should rarely speak in groups unless they are certain of their subject material.

The value of expert power strongly emphasizes how important it is that college and university presidents know the literature of higher education and other fields that relate directly to their presidency. Unfortunately, too many presidents believe that staying in touch with their disciplines is an impressive and striking presidential quality. While remaining current in one's academic discipline may be reassuring and sustaining, the president should quickly become and remain an authority in those fields that relate to the presidential office. As we have established, knowing more about subjects related to the presidency than others know, combined with the office itself, gives an incumbent a decided advantage in virtually any situation. And the president who may not know more than others about a particular subject (and this will be more often than one would prefer) should nevertheless be perceived as knowledgeable. This is why the wise president leaves most details to associates; the president's main job is to inspire, offering an occasional trace of detail merely to imply to others his or her greater knowledge. If you are wrong or mistaken, admit it, but don't make mistakes too often. As the president, except in rare situations, you no longer can afford the self-indulgence of speaking off the top of your head.

Charismatic Power

Charismatic power, the single most effective form of influence, is based on the admiration and liking that people feel for an individual. Some researchers have used the term "referent power" for this category, and others use charismatic. I prefer charismatic, in spite of its sometimes uncomfortable connotations, for it is a more widely understood and used term. This is not the charisma of divine inspiration, a special gift, grace, or talent that some have and most have not, but rather a quality of trust and confidence that virtually any college or university president can honestly cultivate.

To gain the affection, trust, and respect of others has for centuries been viewed by philosophers as the most effective form of leadership. Today, researchers are increasingly able to document that these characteristics referred to as charismatic, or by similar terms, constitute the behavior that is most effective in inspiring others to follow and support a leader (Mott, 1970; Hobbes, 1968; Tedeschi, Schlenker, and Bonoma, 1971; Foa and Foa, 1975; Machiavelli, 1952).

Clearly, someone who is liked and trusted by others is most able to exert influence over them (Tedeschi et al., 1969). A continuous theme throughout history and literature is the person who has become a hero by winning the adulation of others. People identify with these heroes; some go so far as to become worshipful. The way to lead people beyond the limited capacity of more conventional power forms, and even beyond themselves, is to study and learn to use charismatic power ethically. Today, social scientists are documenting and explaining the effective leader's persistent urge to be respected and admired; increasingly, these scholars are realizing that this urge relates more to good management than to ego gratification (McClelland, 1975).

People simply want to agree with and to follow charismatic leaders, often twisting logic to agree with a leader's position. Followers will even defend a charismatic leader when he or she is not present, and will take strong exception to those who are unfairly critical of the leader.

People who follow charismatic leaders are convinced that things will get better, and even feel better about themselves (French and Snyder, 1959). The most mundane job becomes significant.

The leader who combines charismatic power with expert and legitimate power, adding a carefully measured portion of reward power and little or no coercive power, achieves maximum effectiveness. For their part, the followers subjugate their own interests to those expressed by the charismatic leader. In so doing, a symbiotic relatedness is established in which the visions of the leader are translated into physical existence by the collective followers. The personal influence deriving from charismatic power both complements and exceeds the impression made by office, rewards, penalties, and even expertise.

Charisma can often produce results without calling into play other more common methods of power (Barr, 1960; Richman and Farmer, 1974). Most people want to cooperate and to be part of an exciting and potentially significant activity. They simply need a reason to do so, and the leader who takes advantage of all the dimensions of rational charisma provides it. The duration of the leadership depends almost exclusively upon the leader's ability to use charismatic power (Falbo, 1977).

Invariably, then, effective leadership seems to be rooted in charismatic influence rather than in more formal and traditional factors. And this is as valid among highly educated groups like college and university faculties, which assume a peer relationship. Although most academics might presume immunity, sophisticated people are just as prone to succumb to the appeal of power figures, and will often go to ridiculous lengths to gain their acceptance (Jones and Jones, 1964; Hurwitz, Zander, and Hymovitch, 1953). Other high-status figures cooperate and become followers if the charismatic leader can win their commitment and trust (Slusher, Rose, and Roering, 1978).

A seeker of power or a leader who already has a measure of it can sometimes dramatically increase his or her influence by recognizing and responding to the fact that people are attracted to persons of power. Followers are especially loyal if association with a perceived authority figure seems to offer an opportunity to enhance their own reputation or status (Cohen, 1958).

Charismatic influence can be more effectively brought into play in structured rather than unstructured situations (Cohen, 1953, 1959). Attractive personal qualities are less likely to influence behavior in unstructured settings (Pelz, 1951; Godfrey, Fiedler, and Hall, 1959). Structure firmly establishes limits, priorities, and positions. These are optimum conditions for the leader, within which he or she can exercise familiar behavior with those to be led without compromising position or authority.* Structures, however, must come before familiarity. In the analogy of St. Simone, the key is, with warmth and familiarity, to reach *down* from the platform—just don't get off.

By the 1970s, studies had confirmed that a somewhat imprecise mission tends to yield to a leader a comparatively high degree of influence and control over the behavior of a group (Smith, 1973). In spite of failures to achieve specific goals, people may become more accepting, display higher satisfaction, and maintain support for the leader. Vague but lofty goals are good insurance for the leader. Remarkable leaders are often considered persons of great vision. People are more likely to feel comfortable and rewarded and to be supportive if they perceive the leader as both important and somewhat mysterious.

The Development of Charisma

How can charismatic qualities best be developed and used? What is it that makes one person more attractive and appealing than others? Why is it that certain people immediately inspire support, while others with equally good ideas in positions of equal authority fall short? Charisma is the answer.

In spite of the popular impression to the contrary, there is nothing genetic or intuitive about charisma. Anyone of reasonable intelligence and high motivation can develop charismatic characteristics. Age, sex, race, height, weight, and other obvious personal characteristics have little or nothing to do with the ability to develop and use charismatic influence. Virtually anyone can do it.

What creates charisma? Many factors contribute: *sincerity*

---

*Power is structurally determined but also affected by the leader's capacity to convince followers of his or her value and importance. The charismatic leader who inspires trust and confidence can make people feel valuable (Pfeffer, 1981).

appearance, goodness, confidence, wisdom, courage, thought-fulness, kindness, control; but, after reviewing virtually every published study on the subject, I have concluded that the three principal conditions for charisma are distance, style, *and* perceived self-confidence. *And the most clearly docu-mentable of the three charismatic conditions is distance.*

Although it is initially an uncomfortable concept for many, the most certain condition of charisma, *distance,** becomes more acceptable as it is understood (Katz, 1973). Day-to-day intimacy destroys illusions, as anyone familiar with romantic love affairs or the valet-hero relationship—or, for that matter, any presidential assistant—can testify. This is perhaps the main reason why charisma is more difficult to establish at the lower levels of virtually all organizations. The man or woman immediately above you, with whom you work and talk every day, may have many strengths but the frequency of contact obscures these, emphasizes weaknesses, and obliterates charisma. That is why the president's vice presidents and other close associates, in the long run, are perhaps the greatest single test of the presidency.

The leader seen mainly on grand occasions and under special circumstances and who is present often but only briefly at special functions is sufficiently remote to enhance charisma. Every college and university president has this op-portunity, and to let it pass because of modesty or naivete is not merely questionable judgment but a failure of commitment to the presidential role. It is equivalent in spirit to never really accepting the presidency in the first place.

---

*Distance, taken to extreme as a personal lifestyle, can lead to serious problems; but, to the writer's knowledge, there is no significant research that concludes that too much distance is a problem for persons who would be leaders, rather too little. While most leaders are usually talked of as being overly remote and distant, this condition is almost invariably to the advan-tage of the leader, who can then demonstrate his or her unusual humanness by occasional forays into the open; but too many forays make the leader overly familiar to those he or she would lead and, therefore, less the leader. And for purposes of this book for college presidents, who, because of their backgrounds, tend to be more familiar than distant, the values of distance rather than the possible personal problems are emphasized.

Some presidents, particularly at large and complex universities, may allow themselves to be overwhelmed by academic and bureaucratic structures, and if they are unwilling to rise above those structures, become little more than coordinators or in-name-only presidents. They often feel that charisma is impossible in such settings when exactly the opposite is the case. Arthur Schlesinger (1959) and Richard Neustadt (1960) discussed this problem in their analysis of the presidency of the United States, using Franklin Roosevelt as an example of a president who would not allow himself to become a captive of the complexity of the office. The charismatic leader is close enough to the group to permit identification with him or her, but is also perceived as mystical and so somehow a superior figure. It is precisely this that enables people to attach themselves to this personality and then to soar to accomplishment beyond their everyday expectations (Katz, 1973).

On a personal level, the concept of "distance" may seem distasteful. Anyone deliberately using such a stance for personal advantage might seem calculating, cold, and Machiavellian, even dishonest. How can it be right to be less than open, less than completely sharing? Aren't trust and confidence rooted in complete revelation and the exchange of intimate feelings? Quite simply, the answer to these questions is no, not if you would lead or inspire others. Think of the relationship between parent and child, teacher and student, religious leader and congregation, or between intimate friends. Think of the priest who is warm and friendly, but who always remains the priest. Think of those countless relationships that bind human beings together and that involve and even depend on "distance." For leaders to admit full personal parity with those they would lead invites uncertainty, anxiety, confusion, and often chaos. Families, nations, congregations, classrooms have been virtually destroyed for want of respect. For although respect must be earned, it is also a product of values and tradition and is best sustained through "distance." The parent, teacher, the *leader* maintains sufficient proximity to be understanding, and at the same time, sufficient distance to be respected, for familiarity does often breed unproductive controversy. And distance is significant, indeed essential for most, even in a community of peers such as a college or university. It allows the stations (deans, vice presidents, presidents) that have been created by the members (faculty) themselves to maintain reasonable order and insure progress.

A familiar example of the question of distancing and reserve in the social role is that granted to and fostered by religious leaders. The image created as moral, thoughtful, and controlled can be instantaneously jeopardized by one minor lapse in conduct. The successful leader will not allow his office to be devalued, either by himself or by others. If one exceeds the bounds of propriety in the presence of such a person, the demeanor of the effective leader abruptly negates this depreciation (Martin, 1982).

Distance has characterized effective leaders throughout history. And there need be nothing dishonest or unethical in its practice; it is simply unwise for a college president to establish intimate relationships with members of the faculty he or she must serve. I am not suggesting that most presidents won't violate this precept, rather that we are exceedingly fortunate if those intimates don't come back to haunt us in the course of presidential decision making. Distance means being utterly transparent but always remote. Distance is having a close vice-presidential associate after ten years say, "Yes, he's my best friend and I would do virtually anything for him, but I can't say that I completely know him." Distance is recognizing that a leader is no longer "one of the boys or girls." Distance is being a friendly phantom: warm and genuine, concerned and interested, but rarely around too long or overly involved. Distance is recognizing and using the trappings of office, adjusting these only to suit the taste and sophistication of the audience or constituency. Distance balances remoteness with familiarity. The effective leader is both excitingly mysterious and utterly known. Distance is being warm and attentive, open and casual, but never, never really getting off that presidential platform with anyone who knows you as the president.

As long as the leader realizes that he or she is not really very different, if at all, except in perspective, from anyone else, distance will not become arrogance. Indeed, from time to time, an aware leader will laugh at the reassuring thought of his or her own insignificance. There is also a practical reason for this: the leader who takes the image too seriously or becomes overly self-serving will soon be found out and, indeed, will be less effective (McClelland, 1974). In time, he or she will have lost a most vital element in charismatic influence: the trust and confidence of those being led (Schell, 1977). A lack of sincerity or commitment seems invariably to show to those you would inspire; and the message here for college presidents is that if you lose interest in what you are doing, leave.

As the president, you must also remember that the combining forces between the charismatic leader and his or her followers is the establishment of an emotionally charged relationship. Leaders are idealized as those whose strength enables them to assume the responsibility for their followers and who can devise better solutions and direction. Indeed, in this idealization, followers deny that leaders experience doubts, insecurities, or weaknesses. Followers react to their leaders' human foibles with astonishment, dismay, and even anger to an exaggerated degree, as if to say, "If you are not totally dependable, then you may not be dependable at all." Charismatic leaders may drop their reserve safely only with intimates who accept their humanness and who have no motive for placing them in idealized positions or roles of omnipotence (Martin, 1982).

Let's look more closely at the research. Numerous studies have demonstrated the value of both social and psychological distance in effective leadership (Fiedler, 1954, 1955, 1966, 1967; Carp, Vitola, and McLanathan, 1963; Fiedler, O'Brien, and Ilgen, 1969; Burke, 1965; Cleven and Fiedler, 1956; Hawkins, 1962; Hill, 1969; Hunt, 1967; Hutchins and Fiedler, 1960; Julian, 1964). All of these studies support the hypothesis that social distance is positively related to group productivity. Blau and Scott (1962) and Shaw (1965) report that group coherency is strengthened by distance between leader and followers. Stogdill reports Burke's 1965 research, which found that high-need achievement followers with low social distance leaders rated their situations as more tense regardless of the nature of the task. Stogdill then presents twenty-one studies that demonstrate that psychological distance between leader and followers is positively related to group productivity. In other words, productivity tends to be higher under a leader who maintains social and psychological distance between himself or herself and the followers (Stogdill, 1974; Rubin and Goldman, 1968).

In 1955, Shepherd and Weschler found that distance between the leader and followers was associated with fewer communication difficulties. When leaders worked side by side with followers, particularly in formal organizations, greater communication problems resulted. In fact, even authoritarian leaders who are relatively distant are more influential than others. Thiagarajan and Deep (1970) studied three types of leaders—authoritarian, persuasive, and participative—and found the authoritarian most and the participative least powerful. It appears that a combination of a sense of office and a persuasive style result in a leader whom groups tend to follow. It should come as no surprise that followers gain security in association with a strong leader. Individuals are conditioned to respond to clearly defined roles.

People perform more effectively when they like and esteem their leaders (Gottheil and Bielhaber, 1966). Indeed, esteem for the leader is more closely related to performance than esteem of followers for each other. Further, followers like to be liked by high-status figures and will even employ subtle ingratiation techniques (Jones, Gergen, Gempert, and Thibaut, 1965; Jones and Jones, 1964). The higher the perceived status of the leader, the more likely the leader is to be liked and accepted by the group.

Perhaps the study closest to the field of higher education was produced by Seeman (1960), who found that teachers in public schools who rate their principals high in status and perceive wide differences between their own status and that of the principal tend to like and to rate their principals high in effectiveness as leaders. Scott's research suggests that effective leadership and the accomplishment of distance is best achieved when leaders operate less extensively throughout the organization but retain final authority in their own hands (1956).

Style is a related characteristic that distinguishes a leader from the pack, but not so much as to be unsettling. It is not as documentable as distance and is, therefore, more debatable (Stogdill, 1974). Style is a combination of many things—comportment, attitude, speech, dress, mannerisms, appearance, and even personal habits. Style is that fortifying inner sense that allows the leader to be him or herself. Above all else, it does not pander to every popular appetite and fancy, or attempt to be all things to all persons. Style is having sufficient confidence to say occasionally, without checking with even one's closest advisors, "To hell with them; I'm going to be myself."

It is true that with great legitimate power a person can effectively affect virtually any style—regardless of how blatantly. For instance, the person who has so much money that he or she is described and even admired for pecularities in behavior or dress. This may also hold for very distinguished professional/author/artist types. But it rarely applies to college presidents unless you are the president of a most revered institution or you happen to have been extraordinarily distinguished prior to being appointed president. But most shouldn't do it. You must earn respect, confidence, and admiration by more subtle power forms.

Perceived self-confidence is another quality of the charismatic leader: the perception others have that you are self-confident (Stogdill, 1973; Mann, 1959; McClelland, 1970). It relates to a style of speaking and even walking with an air of surety. The effective leader is sufficiently confident to be willing to appoint close associates who are typically superior to him or her. Indeed, usually there is no choice, for such associates are needed to buttress the leader's grand and confident generalizations. Finally, the wise leader remembers that in spite of his or her expertise and wealth of talented advisors, that self-confidence is rooted in human weakness as well as strength, and personal limitations are no less real because of demeanor.

Other conditions that some consider necessary for charisma: Katz (1973) discusses the leader who is charismatic because he or she becomes a symbol of the solution followers wish for to solve internal conflicts. Or, a leader is perceived to have attributes that can advance followers' particular interests. A defensive charisma not only is based on lofty goals, but is a continuation of dependence on a parent. The two conditions necessary for the latter identification are the parent figure's overwhelming power and the inability of the person to escape the exercise of that power (Katz, 1973). Each of these, however, and especially the first two, are products of the leader's effective use of distance, style, and perceived self-confidence, enabling the leader to symbolize hope and advance the interests of his or her people.

Diminishing Charisma

For most, charismatic qualities tend to diminish with time (Fiedler, 1970). The leadership role becomes increasingly difficult because of what appears to be an inevitable progress toward mutual knowledge; most leaders cannot maintain the distance necessary for maximum leadership effectiveness indefinitely. Time and experience tend to take away the mystique. As people come to know their leader, they find a reflection of their own doubts, uncertainties, and limitations, and they are less likely to be as supportive.

While there are a few exceptions to this rule, six to ten years in a particular office is about the maximum for effectively exerting charismatic power. Contrary to popular thought, the smaller and less complex the community, the shorter that term, simply because people come to know their leader faster. (There are some remarkable presidential exceptions to this rule, but the wise president won't generalize from these exceptions.) Typically, after six to ten years, the charismatic leader must rely increasingly on expert power. Unfortunately, too many leaders during this period of decline tend to rely on legitimate or coercive power instead, and as a result, often resign or are forced out of office (Fodor, 1974).

Charismatic leaders can move to other settings and commence the same process all over again, and, assuming genuine interest in these successive positions, may become even more effective. But once charisma is lost or on the wane in a particular setting, regaining it is almost impossible. The wise leader makes plans to move on.

Power and the College Presidency

In reviewing the five forms of power (coercive, reward, legitimate, expert, and charismatic), the college president should bear these things in mind:

1. Underlying all presidential behavior should be a profound and fundamental commitment to goodness, fair play, and improving the condition of the society and all of the people.

2. Generally, charismatic qualities diminish with time, and presidents are inclined to rely too heavily on legitimate and coercive power.

3. The president who uses charismatic power in conjunction with expert and legitimate power, along with a carefully measured portion of reward power, and little or no coercive power, will be most effective.

4. Charisma is created by distance, style, and perceived self-confidence, and the greatest of these is distance. A sincere and deep commitment to a worthy cause or ideal is important, but unfortunately, is not absolutely essential.

5. The higher the perceived status of the president, the most likely he is to be liked and accepted.

6. Idealized qualities of a limitless, magical, unique, and inexplicable nature are ascribed to charismatic leaders by their followers.

7. Charismatic influence is more effective in structured than in unstructured settings.

8. Highly sophisticated people are as attracted to charismatic leaders as are others.

9. Power will be shifted to others if a leader refuses to exert authority, thereby creating a power vacuum.

10. Anyone can be perceived as charismatic.

11. Presidential goals (vision) should be grand but somewhat imprecise, and should be reinforced in various ways in virtually all public settings.

12. The president's greatest single tests will be his or her vice presidents, for they will come to know him or her best.

13. You can rise above your bureaucratic structure!

14. Criticism of nonpresidential staff should be delivered by the appropriate vice president or vice-presidential delegate, and rarely by the president.

15. People will go to unusual lengths to defend charismatic leaders, for they defend the leader's interests as if they were their own.

16. People feel better about themselves and their work and they perform at a higher level when they like and respect their leader.

17. A leader's forecasts will tend to be accepted if the leader is perceived as being an expert.

18. One can be an expert by being knowledgeable about a subject or by being perceived as being an expert.

19. Groups with more than one acknowledged expert are less clear on direction and less effective.

20. Demonstrated expertise tends to legitimize leaders and will grant the leader more security and longer tenure.

21. Once power is legitimized, it no longer depends purely on force of logic or strength for it can stand alone, unless it is abused. In colleges and universities, norms and expectations develop that make the exercise of power expected and accepted (regardless of what some may say). Rather than being a contest of contesting positions, power is made legitimate (department chairs, deans, presidents, etc.) and the corporation can function efficiently and even make progress.

22. Legitimate leaders are more effective when they react less extensively throughout the organization and when they retain final authority.

23. Legitimate leaders who step widely beyond their bounds create unnecessary questions and reservations about their leadership.

24. Appointment to a legitimate position is almost always better than election; hence, an appointed president and an elected faculty leader.

25. The more legitimate one is perceived to be, the more acceptable and effective all other power forms will be (including expert and charismatic). Hence, the important role of governing boards in granting presidential power and the value of inaugurals, academic convocations with appropriate academic pageantry, presidential boxes, formal commencements, and even automobiles and parking spaces.

26. Nonetheless, the president should not forget that people will not willingly follow for long a legitimate leader with whom they don't at least generally agree.

27. The greater the crisis or perceived crisis, the more legitimacy is allowed the leader, hence, the value of real external adversaries and the greater the opportunity for charisma.

28. Leaders who are viewed as cooperative, to a degree

implying softness, by their groups are more likely to be exploited by their groups.

29. A leader should not expect too much from bestowing favors, recognition, promotion, and pay raises; they quickly fade from memory and are replaced by an insatiable expectation of more rewards.

30. If a leader wants to produce long-lasting changes in behavior, it is best to use little or no coercive power, more subtle forms of reward than salary, and to become as legitimate as possible in the view of those the leader would influence.

31. When a leader does not have (or is not granted) sufficient legitimate and reward power, he or she is more inclined to rely on covert and coercive means to obtain ends. The president should have the power to grant privileges, for implicit in this is the right to take them away.

32. The threat of punishment can induce compliance, but it should not be used often.

33. The leader's perceived legitimacy reduces resistance and makes coercion and punishment more acceptable.

34. If a leader is admired, as well as being legitimate, followers will accept punishment more readily.

35. Once punishment is used, it becomes less effective as a power force.

36. When people are allowed or encouraged to relate with one another (common lounges, cafeterias, parties, and other social functions), they are less inclined to respond to leaders who rely heavily on coercive, reward, and legitimate power.

In summary, all the methods of power discussed in this chapter are effective to some degree. From most to least effective for a college or university president, they would probably be ranked as follows: charisma, expert, legitimate, reward, and coercive.*

Finally, the reader should recall that our drive for power and influence is only slightly less intense than our need for food and shelter—we all want to be "somebody." The only variation is one of degree. Our power motives are derived from two prime sources: (1) personal aggrandizement, which requires exploitation of others, and (2) the need to influence others' behavior for the common good, which conveys a broader benefit. Nonetheless, both personal motives gain more effective results than virtually all others. It is both assumed and believed that the vast majority of college presidents are motivated by the second—the common good.

I have tried in this chapter to reduce the sometimes uncomfortable and always incomplete words of research to an ineffable leadership style in order to suggest a leadership design that could be considered by college presidents. I have sought to be both true to the research and sensitive in its rendering and interpretation, and it is from this delicate dichotomy that I proceed to the following chapters. Throughout these chapters, the reader should bear in mind the research cited in this chapter, for, in significant measure, they represent the author's attempt, in fact or retrospect, to test and use this research during almost a decade as a college president.

* Be a friendly phantom.

* Learn to be everywhere and nowhere.

* Be absolutely accessible but always remote.

---

*For application to higher education, Richman and Farmer's book, *Leadership, Goals and Power in Higher Education*, presents nineteen sources of power and influence in a college or university. To document their conclusions, they cite eight studies conducted from 1964 through 1974 (Richman and Farmer, 1974). Of the nineteen sources of power, nine have to do with charismatic, three with expert, five with legitimate, two with coercive, and none with reward power.

* Be different. If you can't, do something else.
* Walk with confidence.
* Never forget where you came from.

CHAPTER 4

The Charismatic Presidency

The power which erring men call chance.
                                    John Milton

Charisma is that wonderful quality of being taken more seriously than you deserve.

                                    Kenneth Shaw

BECAUSE OF THE REQUISITES of leadership and the limits that boards, bureaucrats, laws, and academic tradition have placed on presidential power, a president may wish to consider various means of increasing his or her charismatic influence. Indeed, in many settings, it is literally all the president has. The president is expected to lead thousands with little but an ability to inspire confidence, trust, and hope.

At the core of any effort to increase charismatic influence must be commitment, sincerity, goodness, and caring. Most would agree that presidents who are unsuccessful fail mainly from an inability to get outside themselves. Without these human qualities, a quest for charisma can become a transparent exercise in vanity.

The President's Vision

Unless the president articulates a special vision, mission, or cause for the institution, he or she will not be viewed as a true leader. A mission is grand and all-embracing, and includes

57

lofty, humanistic concepts like peace, progress, freedom, and the welfare of the community and greater public as well as the special mission for the institution. Don't be afraid to dream and to share that dream—it will even inspire you. Lofty and sometimes rather vague goals promote morale and leadership effectiveness, so long as the goals are legitimate and progress toward their achievement is made. It is perhaps worthwhile to note that George Gallup observed, "People tend to judge a man by his goals, by what he's trying to do, and not necessarily by what he accomplished or how well he succeeds" (Edelman, 1964). Pruitt's study comparing effective with typical college and university presidents concluded that the former had a "mission" or "vision" that seemed to radiate from them (1976). Although important for all, a special presidential vision is especially important for small, liberal arts colleges and regional public institutions (two- and four-year). Within such situations, people need a more significant collective identity, a sense of pride that tends to inspire both new heights and sacrifices for a greater common cause.

The president who appears to have achieved a personal integration and higher purpose and can articulate it for others becomes a charismatic figure (Katz, 1973). Father Theodore Hesburgh has written about the mission of an institution (Fisher, 1980):

> The most important contribution a president can make to institutional advancement is to articulate his vision of the institution so persistently and persuasively that it becomes shared by all constituencies, internal and external, who adopt it as their own. Whatever else he is clear and enthusiastic about, the president must most of all elaborate his specific vision, rethink it as times change, perfect it as he learns from experience, and make his contribution to an evolving sense of institutional purpose.

Your vision should consider the desires and the nature of both external and internal constituents:

> We will become the finest institution of our kind in America, an institution whose faculty members truly care about students and

their dreams, an institution that will nurture and provide opportunities for free and full expression . . . that will significantly contribute to enabling our society to realize its ultimate potential.

Remember, this is the time to dream.

Not infrequently, the presidential vision is confused with a more prosaic long-range plan and specific goals involving many faculty, administrative staff, and students. No one becomes excited about a detailed 120-page mission statement. It is fine to put together a planning group as a follow-up activity, but its precursor and inspiration should be the president's concise, exciting mission statement, which initially always includes a brief statement about the good work of his or her predecessor, but most importantly, stating his or her personal vision for the institution and its people. Initially, an informal refinement of these aspirations for close and valued associates is appropriate; but the public announcement should not be the product of a committee or any other campus group—it should be the president's.

The dream should be repeated on every possible occasion, to remind both the president and the campus. And once the mission is settled on, it should not change dramatically. People can absorb only so many dreams and so much inspiration. Although the president may tire of repeating the vision, the campus won't tire of hearing it so long as its presentation is reasonable, sincere, and accomplished.

Don't Take Your Myth Seriously

Assuming that these things are done well, a legend or myth soon begins to grow around the president. The myth is the license to continue providing the inspiration needed to fulfill the president's high expectations for everyone on campus, including him or herself. Becoming hostage to extraordinary goals, everyone will achieve more than they—or the president—ever expected. People outside the institution will begin to expect exceptional things, things that will sometimes appear impossible, but the president will often accomplish them. The myth, of course, will be bigger than the real people or institution; the myth can grow so long as the president does not take it seriously or accept it as fact.

The words of Dag Hammarskjold seem appropriate:

> Around a man who has been pushed into the limelight, a legend begins to grow as it does around a dead man. But a dead man is in no danger of yielding to the temptation to accept his legend as reality. I pity the man who falls in love with his image as it is drawn by public opinion. (1965)

The fabric of the myth will be the impressions of the people the president would lead and influence, reflecting their dreams, hopes, and aspirations also. They provide the moral rationale for continued strength and progress.

Act Like the President

The charismatic president acts like a president. This is difficult, for most of us are never sure that we are worthy of the office, and sometimes convinced that we aren't. In the earlier days, before social mobility in the United States, it must've been easier, for most presidents were literally born to office and could be more comfortably impervious to their own limitations. Effective leaders are self-confident, have an evident sense of identity and personal style, and understand that structure and organization contribute to effective leadership. The president carries the office and its trappings with assurance, neither apologetically nor with condescension. A matter-of-fact attitude and unspoken confidence toward personal accomplishments and attributes, and a forgiving spirit toward petty criticisms should characterize the president. The little things that are often uncomfortable to do, matter; for example, it's a good idea to use drivers and have doors opened. The modest response to those who address the president by title, "Just call me Bob or Jane," is not always appropriate. A modest "Aw shucks" attitude is all right if it is not carried too far. The key is to be warm, kind, beneficent, and even a bit folksy while firmly situated on the presidential platform; once again, just don't get off that platform.

Speaking Engagements and Ceremonies

Take advantage of and plan for speaking engagements and ceremonies. To do otherwise is amateur theater. While the purpose is to impress the audience, the greater goal is to enhance the presidency and the special mission of the institution. Ceremonies provide occasions to mobilize support and quiet opposition (Pfeffer, 1981). Even the physical settings for appearances are important (Peters, 1978). The size, location, and configuration of the physical space provide the backdrop against which the president makes the presentation and thereby influences its interpretation and effects. Whether the occasion is a faculty meeting or a commencement, reverberations from any ceremony should be positive, for as long as any president is in office he or she is the institution, in spite of personal modesty or collegial inclinations. Remember that a leader's influence is significantly based on the group's acceptance of some kind of code or standard (French and Raven, 1959). Few things reinforce academic traditions more effectively than ceremonies and sensitively planned presentations on campus.

Don't accept all speaking engagements on campus. This insures that the president will stay in demand for years, and that the extent of his or her off-campus activities will be recognized. What most students and faculty really mean when they say, "We wish we could see more of the president," is that they really need a president and that they appreciate the president's off-campus activities on their behalf (Benezet et al., 1981). Research also indicates that overexposure is killing. A brief but impressive introduction prepared by the president's assistant or public-relations officer can be helpful. (Pomposity is also out; Mr. or Madam President is not appropriate.) But however well the audience knows the president, an introduction is important. According to recent studies in forensics, an impressive talk should begin behind an elevated rostrum located several yards from the audience. Later, to move from behind the rostrum is a gesture of warmth and informality. Some professors are absolute masters of this technique. Presentations in halls that can barely contain the crowd are more moving.

Any speech should begin with brief remarks about the state of the college or university and how that relates to the president's (and their) special mission or vision; the president is always the president, even if the subject is ornithology, and both the speaker and the audience need to be reminded of that fact. It is important that the special mission of the president's administration, whenever appropriate, be kept before the community. Question and answer periods after the presentation are usually a bad idea. A preferable alternative is to adjourn the meeting and answer individual questions at the podium. This permits the speaker to be open and interested in reactions but avoids the possibility of contrary and distracting speeches from the audience. The president can no longer enjoy the luxury of spontaneous brilliance or foolishness. Good presidential speeches are interesting, informative, and most of all, inspiring. Speeches to be delivered to large audiences or very important groups should be written out. This shows seriousness about the occasion, prevents misstatements, and makes it easy to distribute copies to faculty, staff, students, and the media. If the president is a poor speech maker, lessons are in order.

Although most campus appearances are relatively informal, traditional, formal ceremonies can lend much to the presidential aura. The president's legitimate power usually extends to ceremonials and should be used. Ceremonies like inaugurals, commencements, installations, orientations, and even banquets should be professionally and carefully arranged to enhance the presidency; the more medieval pageantry, the better. Pressures to simplify or democratize these programs excessively can be warded off; there are all kinds of unselfish reasons to be cited, such as authorities who indicate that ceremonies and tradition build morale and increase alumni loyalty and support for the institution. The distance that diffident yet dramatic flair can give is crucial.

In retrospect, I wish that I had given more thoughtful attention to my inauguration. Inaugurals are excellent occasions to solidify and institutionalize presidential power (Pfeffer, 1981). The inauguration can include an investiture ritual that further ratifies the importance of the office. These occasions almost automatically attract media attention and are an important way to broadcast the president's vision. Wide attendance at the inauguration, if it can be arranged without the appearance of authoritarianism, is valuable. Take pains to attract as many students, faculty members, trustees, legislators, and influential community leaders as possible.

The trappings of office—a presidential chain and medal, distinctive though not gaudy presidential cap and gown, a mace carried by an associate—should be made the most of. The president should always deliver a brief and inspiring message at any ceremonial function on campus.

For commencements, usually only flagship schools are able to arrange a "name" commencement speaker. This is all the better; the president can be the speaker. And if you have an outside speaker, always send informational materials about the institution and, most particularly, your last state-of-the-institution address. The discerning speaker will always want to include local color in an address and should be encouraged to do so. In any case, the commencement program should always include a brief president's charge to the graduates. If the president is not especially creative, an assistant or public-relations officer can come up with a helpful draft for use at campus ceremonies. The chief academic officer or another vice president or staff member, never the president, should preside; the president should be introduced for a brief inspiring message.

The Legitimate Adversary

Identifying a legitimate off-campus adversary or issue around which to rally the campus will give the president's standing a special boost. The key word is legitimate. A legitimate controversy unites the campus and lessens the natural inclination to throw rocks at the president when local problems inevitably occur. The external issue must relate to achieving the objectives of members of the campus community (Katz, 1973). When an issue begins to wear thin, find another. And, if the issue is legitimate, don't be overly concerned about offending off-campus power forces. In the final analysis, the most important constituency for a college president is the campus—faculty, students, and staff.

In the process, an inspiring rationale for the president's action and plans is essential. What amounts to a ringing call for continued support and commitment as well as candid, honest confirmation of legitimate and formidable off-campus opposition should issue from the president's office. Neither indictments nor even criticism of individuals is wise. It insures permanent enemies and colors the president's image with pettiness. When you take issue, take issue with questionable ideas, practices, concepts, institutions, and the like—not with individuals. Never attack individuals, even when they attack you.

Katz (1973) provides an interesting discussion on the value of an inspiring rationale and using an external adversary in comparing two American presidents, Franklin D. Roosevelt and Harry S. Truman. Both espoused the cause of the common people vigorously and built effective links with them. Truman did not take the process far beyond simply creating the links. The common man believed that Truman genuinely represented the people's interests but was himself a common man. "In Roosevelt, however, we had a leader whose power in the eyes of the people to achieve great things was almost unlimited" (Katz, 1973). Why? Roosevelt knew about organizations. He granted federal agencies sufficiently overlapping responsibility and appointed strong personalities as agency heads. This allowed him to be the natural arbiter and ultimate decision maker. The Great Depression and World War II further encouraged the people to regard him as a charismatic figure.

The Value of Diversions

Honest diversions for faculty and students—sports events, lectures, plays, competitions, and so on—are important and healthy and should be fostered by the president. These outlets defuse pent-up emotion, anger, and threats—the president's, as well as everyone else's. If the number of outlets available is maximized, there should be sufficient opportunity for everyone to engage in attractive and worthwhile activities. These also give people a chance to excel and share the trappings of prestige in constructive ways.

Although a community of intellectuals is rarely demonstrative, when the president is in danger or trouble, they will come through in ways that are both reassuring and touching. Students will say, as they did of Robert G. Bone at Illinois State, "If the president knew about that leaky shower, it would be fixed." Faculty will say, as they did of Herman Wells at Indiana, "The president is our voice." Trustees, benefactors, politicians, public figures, bureaucrats, alumni, and parents will respect and admire the president. The media will write and talk about the president. Straining to be what the campus and community think they see, in the process, you will become so much more than you thought you could be.

Adversaries

There are always those who are just waiting for the president to fail. This is only natural; front runners are watched and criticized as well as admired and envied (MacEoin, 1976). Some in the wings would like to replace the actor on center stage, or, at the very least, to see the actor displaced. Any advocate of change, at least initially, loses the support of representatives of the established order; in time, detractors will literally have no choice in the matter, and many will become enthusiastic supporters.

Open adversaries will be far easier to handle than more subtle denigrators—those "friends" such as less successful college presidents, a few trustees, most politicians, occasionally staff, and most others competing for attention in the same arena. They envy success and anyone who appears to do things more quickly or more effectively than themselves. Those are the people who will say: "It takes a while," or "Be very careful before you act," or "It's best not to rock the boat," or "If you take the king's gold, you are the king's man." They will always counsel moderation and inaction and quote Aristotle, in this case incorrectly, of course. They will be the ones who will invariably recommend a "cooperative" style as the best way to change and improve conditions. They will say, "The Church has always been that way, so you might as well reconcile yourself to it," and in public higher education, "State systems are here to stay, so why question their effectiveness?" They will extol more "effective communication" as the key to better times. (Not that anyone really knows for sure what "more effective communication" is or how people who achieve such a grand condition feel.) Of course, better communication is important, both on and off campus, but be wary of those who speak of it constantly.

In time, an effective president who does not overly personalize conflict will find most enemies deciding that it is wiser to be an ally, and some may even become fast and staunch supporters. In one instance, a state budget analyst for higher education who had initially turned livid at the very mention of the name of an assertive state-university president, later became so enthusiastic that he taught part-time on the university faculty and donated his entire salary to the university foundation—and urged the president to run for governor. Patience will win them all, and on your terms.

Demagogues, Zealots, and Martyrs

A word of warning: beware of demagogues, zealots, and martyrs. Such people invariably inflict as much harm on their friends as on their opponents. Unless they are completely in violation of institutional policy or laws, grant them their missionary activities. Yes, they will gain some support, at least temporarily. But, unless there is absolutely no acceptable alternative, it is a mistake to provoke or engage them in debate, for they usually have nothing to lose. With neither respect for authority nor appreciation for charisma, as true zealots, they are beyond rational discussion. Issues are often only pretexts for recognition. They will seek to take everything anyone has to offer and demand more, and, in the end, can completely undermine the president's authority.

Ignore zealots if possible; if not, shunt them off on an associate whom you can later protect. If all else fails and their popular support is gaining, an insignificant issue can be granted to them, allowing the president to earn the support of the greater public so long as the move does not appear to be made out of weakness.

Certain trustees are also best given a wide berth. Threatening to resign when trustees are vexatious and provoking runs the risk of appearing foolish and that the resignation will be accepted. The president who leaves should do so on his or her own terms. The best way to handle unreachable trustees is, to whatever extent possible, with a polite avoidance; and never give up on the prospect of conversation. Behind-the-scenes machinations against them with other trustees will only reduce the president's perceived self-confidence in the eyes of trustees who are supportive. Do not engage in gossip about anyone for any reason.

Conflict

Conflict, however, has its value (Katz, 1973; Stogdill, 1974). The very organization of a college or university invites conflict. Contained conflict can inspire healthy competition and produce more impressive results. It allows the president occasionally to redefine the limits of his or her delegates' authority, in the process elevating the presidential office. Perfect harmony is among the first signs of an unhealthy, dying organization, or one so structured that important work cannot be done. With no overlap, there is no tension, and without tension, there is neither movement nor constructive activity—and little need for a president. If the tension is in check, but there nonetheless, and a spirit of cooperation along with a sense of grand mission is instilled, the institution will neither "blow up" nor go to sleep.

Overexposure and Committee Meetings

How the president spends time has an important bearing on his or her charisma. It is established that overexposure can be extremely disadvantageous to a leader's effectiveness. Because of their backgrounds or personal anxiety or both, some presidents seem bent on attending all meetings and representing themselves in virtually all important negotiations. Presidential membership on official committees, whether on campus or off, is almost always counterproductive or a waste of time. With precious few exceptions, spending two or three hours in a meeting waiting for a turn to talk cannot be justified. Most damaging, however, is the tendency of participation to turn the president into one of the people he or she is trying to lead, and to reduce the leader's effectiveness and ability to communicate (Shepherd and Weschler, 1955; Carp, Vitola, and McLanahan, 1963). Participation also unnecessarily risks the possibility of making unwise statements. Instead, the president should send a trusted and able delegate and stay in touch with the delegate. This produces much better results. Although in the beginning, people will earnestly press you to be a member of an "important" committee, if you equivocate and later assign a delegate, they will soon desist. Finally, people come to like this system better because it gives everyone on campus someone to petition—you.

The Fundamental Importance of the People

Of course, the foundation of campus charisma is the extent to which the president stays in touch with the people, the campus constituency—students, faculty, and lower-level support staff like housekeepers, cooks, and maintenance workers. To do this, these people must know that the president sincerely cares about them and their welfare. Many of these people will continue to support the president enthusiastically, even in the midst of exceedingly controversial activities or mistakes. Years ago, Weber wrote of the "magic aura" that people attribute to such leaders, willingly overlooking personal weaknesses (1947). The leader is one of them, but apart from them, a visible and friendly phantom. Occasionally, the president stops for coffee and personal words about family and friends, but does not discuss work or campus politics at length.

This sense of identification of people with the president can be more important than the actual distribution of rewards and privileges. They know that the president cares and realizes that they are contributing to the institutional mission. The faculty will work harder, their teaching will be of the highest quality, the campus will look better, and the food will be tastier—all delivered with a smile and a sense of purpose. The campus is simply a great place to be, and the president is the epitome of what a leader should be—"Our President."

Visit every building on campus regularly and know where the coffee pots are. The president should be seen walking around the campus during class breaks, joining students for drinks at the campus social center. (Walk up and ask to join them.) Set aside a time each week for student drop-in office hours. It doesn't matter whether there are 500 or 50,000 students enrolled; the president still needs to see students and vice versa; no business is more pressing. Similarly, it is wise to invite randomly selected groups of faculty to the office occasionally for discussion. The object is to stay in touch.

An ideal way to maintain close constituent relations is to be present during periods of exceptional difficulty or great joy in the lives of faculty, students, or staff. It is better to miss a board meeting than a funeral. People will always remember that the president attended the wedding of a student. To visit a custodian in the hospital is not only thoughtful and cheering but will do more to offset ill feelings during periods of contract negotiations than the highest-paid negotiator. These things should be done regularly, not just when your leadership is shaky. To share in the delicious joy of an athletic championship or the birth of a child is a feeling that binds leader and followers together in a way that will insure people's loyalty through minor difficulties and great catastrophes, and will contribute immensely to their confidence. If the president has done his or her job, it will be students and workers—the so-called "little people"—whose support will persist, even when the president has made a mistake, and it is they who will really make the job worthwhile.

Faculty and staff salaries and benefits warrant another word here. There is the temptation, especially when off campus or in cloistered board rooms, to compromise the interests of those on campus. It would be easy to give in to the pressures of political expediency voiced by some trustees, public figures, alumni, and, in public institutions, systemwide officers, politicians, and state bureaucrats. But, within reason, the president's job is to take care of the people; if the president says one thing off campus, and another thing on campus, then he or she will soon be found out. The president's interests, as well as those of the sponsoring body, are better served if the prime denominator of the institution's health and vitality is the specific and measurable (salaries and benefits) as well as the less tangible rewards paid to faculty and staff. The leader who takes care of people will be taken care of, and gladly granted executive privilege.

* Have a vision. Stand for something.

* Think, talk, and walk like a president; smile and laugh and be especially nice to the "little" people.

* Get to know the cooks, the custodial force, and the maintenance people. They're the least complicated and most open people on the campus and, in times of difficulty, the most supportive.

* Don't give too many speeches on campus.

* Zealots are irrational and unafraid; either assign them to someone else or let them run their course.

* Remember that even the most self-righteous are motivated by self-interest.

* Take regular walks around campus.

* Direct your thoughts and control your emotions, but use both.

* Get a personal assistant with whom you can blow off steam.

* Believe in yourself or no one else can.

* Your people rightfully expect you to be strong; never, never discuss your problems with them.

* Keep your distance.

* The test of whether you're any good is not how you treat the mighty but how you treat those who work for you, especially the most humble.

* If you have to remind people who you are, you aren't.

* Don't make excuses, and don't make the same mistake twice.

* If possible, take the center seat.

* The president who takes a strong and irrevocably certain position is usually wrong.

* Never admit you're tired except to your secretary, your assistant, and your spouse.

CHAPTER 5

The President and the Administration

The highest proof of virtue is to possess boundless power without abusing it.

Thomas Babington, Lord Macaulay, 1843

Power is pleasure; pleasure sweetens pain.
William Hazlitt, 1826

WHAT FOLLOWS is an examination of college and university administration that focuses on the research in leadership and power and the author's personal experience in the presidency. There are unquestionably other effective organizational administrative and presidential styles than those assumed in this chapter, as well as other appropriate applications of the research.

What is unique about this discussion, however, is the deliberate association of research, which has been tested, at least largely, in personal experience and is presented in that light. Before proceeding, the reader should bear in mind the conclusions reached in Chapter 2 about leadership and especially in Chapter 3 about power. Further, this presentation is based on the conviction that regardless of an institution's systems and management designs, it will not operate as effectively as it should—and may operate disastrously—unless the president knows and appreciates the characteristics and techniques of leadership and power.

The leadership vacuum in higher education today was considered earlier. Perhaps, as some have suggested, no more can be expected of a society in transition where traditional leadership models are questioned and research on the subject is largely ignored. However, a thesis of this book is that leadership and the attempt to influence are immutable factors in human social behavior, virtually the same in all times and all societies. While the style and superficial characteristics of effective leadership and power wielding may change because cultures and situations vary, they remain essentially the same.

Power and the Administration

Inside the university, substantial legitimate power is usually available to the president with regard to administrative staff; this is probably the only campus relationship for which this is the case. Reward power and coercive power with administrators are best used sparingly by the president, and except in rare instances, only with those who report directly to the president.

The administration should be viewed as mission oriented, dynamic, and enlightened. More than any other segment of the academic community, the administration—under its charismatic president's inspired direction—should seem unified. The president's job is always to appear inspired, despite any personal feelings to the contrary—and contrary feelings will emerge at some times.

All administrators should be the president's and be seen that way, for it is through the administration that the president's legitimate authority can be most obvious and effective and therefore be conveyed to others outside the administration. Administrators should not hold tenure (as administrators), and astute boards do not include them on presidential search committees. While it is best that administrators be systematically evaluated every two to four years by the president's office, this process must not convey the message that the administrator in question is accountable to those being asked to evaluate the administrator. This mistake can lead to a campus full of demagogues competing with the president, disloyal or autonomous administrators, and a frustrated president. Administrators work for and report to the president; lines of authority should be clearly defined, with sufficiently overlapping responsibilities to insure that important areas are not overlooked (Burke, 1966; Katz, 1973; Caplow, 1968). Some overlapping in administrative responsibilities also contributes to a productive state of dynamic tension and an occasional opportunity for you to arbitrate disputes, thus reinforcing the importance of the presidential office. Under optimal conditions, administrators have but three choices: to support the president, change his or her mind, or resign. The president should openly and candidly convey this concept of administration to all administrative officers and the entire campus community, preferably during the first weeks after appointment. While it is more uncomfortable for presidents of some tenure to announce this condition, it nonetheless should be done, but after giving careful thought to methodology. If a comfortable strategy fails to emerge, the announcement should simply be issued anyway. It is important to stick to this policy and not slip back into old patterns of collegiality.

The House-Appointed President

This concept of presidential authority, difficult for most presidents, is even more so—and more essential—for persons appointed to the presidency from within an institution. The latter presidency is bound to be more challenging because it is so difficult to achieve the distance necessary to exercise charismatic leadership; people know you too well. There have been many ineffective "house-appointed" presidents who very probably would have been effective someplace else. Some people can make the transition from faculty or administrative post to the presidency of the same institution, but not many. The successful emergent president is often found in the small private college where a single individual occasionally emerges as an effective leader, a figure around whom virtually all forces of the institution converge and who therefore is uniquely qualified to assume the presidency. If you are this type, fine; if not, go back and reread Chapter 3 very carefully. Some institutions have the questionable policy of appointing the academic vice president or provost who will succeed to the presidency. Nevertheless, most presidents have a better chance if they have been appointed from the outside. Although not born to the presidency, at least they do not carry the burden of past intimacies into the president's office.

Presidential Associates

A crucial factor is the president's working relationship with people whose talent and intelligence are, at least latently, superior to his or her own. To be surrounded by persons of lesser ability or potential is to invite the burden of incompetence and, ultimately, of failure. The temptation is great because it is much easier to play king or queen with people of less ability, but such reigns are usually both unsuccessful and short. It is also important that the president share the credit for successes, the lion's part, with subordinates, faculty, students, and trustees, and, at the same time, be willing to take virtually all the responsibility for failures. This may not be fair but it is a must. During periods of difficulty, associates should be so able that the president seeks their counsel, not out of courtesy but out of respect for their judgment. Indeed, Berkowitz and Daniels (1963) found that if a leader both shares credit for success and conveys his or her dependence on staff, people will admire the leader more and be more productive. Staff produce less and dislike a leader more to the extent to which they are made to feel responsible for failures.

Administrative Organization

A high degree of administrative organization and structure is implicit in this style (Burke, 1966; Caplow, 1968). This is most especially true for charismatic leaders, since they must maintain a sensitive distance from those they would lead and manage. Ordinarily, there should be from three to five line divisions* of a college or university, with the exception of some large and complex multiversities, and the president will have from one to three staff assistants. Only under very unusual circumstances should there be an executive vice president (more on this later).

Close Associates and Presidential Distance

To preserve presidential influence and authority, the distance between the president and his or her closest associates should be kept clear. However, you will probably not follow this advice in all cases, as I did not. Intimacy with close associates invites unproductive tension and can reduce productivity, morale, and admiration for the leader. As already suggested, perhaps the president's greatest test is to maintain the leadership role with these associates. They know the president best and so are most likely to exploit that relationship and challenge presidential authority, usually in the name of friendship and support. Associates should feel a kind of respectful anxiety toward the president. Neither they nor anyone else on campus should ever know, or even think they know, the president's innermost thoughts. The day a president starts telling his or her real problems to vice presidents is the day he or she should begin planning to move on. Do not be hesitant to dismiss or reassign someone who persists in closing the distance. Otherwise, it will only be a matter of time before the presidential territory is completely occupied by your closest confederates—and it will be too late to act.

---

*Line officers are those who have other professionals reporting to them; staff officers report to line officers and have no professionals reporting to them.

Socializing with Staff and the Role of the Spouse

Warmth and consideration should characterize the president's relations with the staff. Rarely is it wise to throw around presidential weight, but when you do, mean it.

Socializing with staff should be restricted to rare occasions. This is not to say that it is wrong to socialize with staff, but the astute president will remember that studies clearly demonstrate that too much informal behavior on the part of leaders tends to reduce both their legitimacy and their effectiveness. Where to draw the line is a personal matter, but the natural tendency is to err on the side of the familiar. By rarely extending or accepting purely social invitations, the president will gently discourage overtures. People will not like you less but rather respect you more. Socialize more with outsiders.

If you have a spouse, it is better not to involve him or her rather than to risk excessive entanglement. Undue involvement by spouses can, and often does, lead to unspoken and unidentifiable problems between you and your staff, and finally, between you and your spouse. It can get to the point where you can't honestly hold your delegates accountable for their areas of responsibility; and who is going to tell the president that his or her spouse is a pain? (And if they do, how are you going to relate with them in the future and, more importantly, how are you going to inform your spouse?) Although there are some remarkable exceptions, the ideal spouse for a leader is a cameo, and since this is considered by many an unacceptable form of tokenism today, little more than appearance at the president's side can be asked. If this isn't acceptable to the spouse, the president should do the job and let the spouse pursue his or her own career. With most spouses it is neither fair nor wise to expect more. Several national presidential associations (the Council of Independent Colleges and the American Association of State Colleges and Universities, for example) have helpful material and even conferences on the role of the spouse, and often their advice is more positive than this position.

Frequently entertaining vice presidents and spouses is a

waste both of time and institutional money and will automatically reduce the president's charismatic qualities. Since vice presidents talk about presidents anyway, why give them more to talk about?

Close Friends and Intimacy

Employing close friends who report directly to you is probably a mistake. Although there are rare exceptions, intimate friends usually make better confidantes than subordinates. Genuine friendships with close advisors are fine; to put up with a strong president, they will have to like him or her. But to retain the leadership role, the president must insure that those friendships retain a measure of mystique and objectivity. This will probably be impossible for you, as it was for me, but at least you should know that this course is advisable. Adolph Berle puts it this way: "One of the first impacts (upon assuming office) is realization that the obligations of power take precedence over other obligations formerly held nearest and dearest. A man in power can have no friends in the sense that he must refuse to the friend considerations, that power aside, he would have accorded" (Berle, 1967). But in reality, some advisors will be closer than others. Avoid any favoritism, for these relationships are known or suspected by all. Indeed, usually the close associate pays the price of friendship; the president should be so careful that the associate earns fewer rewards and more pressure because of the relationship.

Similarly, it is generally best not to establish intimate friendships with the same people whose influence you seek. You will need your mystique with them also. Nonetheless, you will probably make some exceptions, and with luck, those friendships won't jeopardize the accomplishment of your vision. Close friends tend to want to debate decisions, even after the time for debate is over, when what the leader needs is to gain the support of important people.

The presidency is, by nature, a lonely position, and its incumbent needs someone to turn to. The temptation is to turn to close associates, family, and friends. To become overly fa-

miliar with close associates can compromise the leader's effectiveness with them as well as with others. Taking problems
home can make the office an impossible full-time job that
yields no respite and often a troubled marriage. Although
close friends off campus can be sympathetic, they seldom
know enough to be helpful. A presidential assistant can help
but is rarely able to be completely objective. Many presidents
find national meetings and special conferences sources of
rejuvenation and a setting for complete candor. Other presidents, regardless of their personal style, understand the
problems of the office, and talking to one who is not in direct
competition with you can provide consolation and even advice. It's helpful just to be able to talk to someone who understands. Perhaps the most consistently valuable places for
presidential catharsis and inspiration are the increasing
number of special conferences and meetings offered for presidents by national professional associations: American Association of State Colleges and Universities (AASCU); American
Council on Education (ACE); Association of Governing Boards
(AGB); Council of Independent Colleges (CIC); Council for Advancement and Support of Education (CASE); and others. At
such conferences, there is reasonable assurance of objectivity,
understanding, occasionally helpful advice, and, most of all,
enlightened honest company.

The Key Role of Top Associates

If the president appoints superior persons to top positions,
they are the prime agents in accomplishing institutional goals.
Their task is to implement effectively the president's plans
and dreams, which they have helped to shape. A good president will always demand and continually press for more from
top associates and advisors. The degree to which they remain
committed depends almost entirely on the president's relationship with them. That relationship should maximize their
contributions and minimize their incursions into presidential
domain. Support them, comfort them, inspire them, and at the

same time keep them a bit anxious and wary. The president provides legitimate favors, opportunities to cultivate their own leadership styles and mystique, and rewards for good performance in the form of salary and perquisites. Although at least tacit support can often be bought from potential or real campus adversaries, taking care of associates is primary. Never take them for granted.

Loyalty

As far as the administrative staff as a whole is concerned, loyalty is as important as competence. The only way to deal with disloyalty is to discharge the person. To tolerate even the slightest disloyalty from an administrative subordinate is to set a shorter time limit on an effective presidency.

Vice presidents, as well as other administrative staff, serve only at the pleasure of the president. Loyalty is as important as competence, and repeated erosion of presidential territory is a form of disloyalty, albeit unconscious.

This obligation of loyalty *does not* hold for faculty and students; the opposite is true. For a president to have maximum charismatic influence within a college or university community, faculty and students should be relatively unfettered to insure that their representations are relatively uninhibited and candid, and in the process, test the administration. And of course, in an academic community, it is neither acceptable nor realistic to expect such compliance from nonadministrative staff.

Coalitions

Watch out for coalitions. To attempt to gain support from others at the president's expense is a more serious act of disloyalty than a direct challenge to authority. When subordinates form a coalition against the president, they must go—and in a way that discourages anyone else from even thinking of the same tactics. If a person cannot be gotten rid of, a way should be found to treat him or her openly as an adversary, which after a while will bring his or her resignation, assuming that other subordinates are loyal.

Those Who Denigrate Your Predecessor

An administrator who denigrates your predecessor is untrustworthy; you will be his next object. By discharging or returning that person to the faculty, the president will have made an example—probably the only one necessary—of an adversary. But the president who is lucky and enters office stating strongly and candidly that loyalty is expected may not have to use any examples at all.

New Administrators

From time to time, the president will need new administrative staff. Bear in mind the possible need for new associates whenever meeting new people. Although bright, well-educated, enthusiastic, outgoing, and assertive people are usually harder to handle, they do a magnificent job if they are inspired. If experience is not too costly, look for that too. (Here again, be wary of the person who speaks critically of a former employer.)

An Executive Vice President

Having a clearly designated second in command is a questionable practice; there is room for only one on the presidential platform. The only time to consider appointing an executive vice president is when you feel your internal effectiveness is exhausted, but you have some external mileage left and are not inclined to look for another position. Then an appropriate second in command would be a trusted and able associate of long standing. Even so, any contrary forces that develop on the campus may use this person as a rallying point against the incumbent. This is one reason why ancient emperors frequently waited until they were on their deathbeds to name their successors. The preferable plan is to delegate responsibility and authority equally to several individuals. Ordinarily, none should be "more equal" than the others. In their absence, some presidents find it effective to form a group comprised of the vice presidents but chaired by an assistant to make necessary decisions. If a vice president is designated to be in charge during the president's absence, the equality of all vice presidents should be stressed during presidential staff meetings.

Administrative Salaries

Administrators should be paid as much as conditions allow, and their salaries based on merit as much as possible, and they should know that this is the policy. It is best, however, to keep private the amount each is paid (Pfeffer, 1981). Instead of inviting contention over the validity of salary rewards, many organizations outside higher education have adopted a policy of being very selective about releasing salary information—a good model for college and university presidents.

The Presidential Assistant

A loyal and able assistant can be the president's most important staff member. He or she belongs to you, for the assistant's role is defined exclusively in terms of your best interests. Without the president, the assistant has no professional existence. A good assistant performs everything from the menial to the magnificent: running errands, opening doors, driving to off-campus meetings, representing the president, and at times, acting as vice president without portfolio. The assistant must be so sensitive that there is not the slightest appearance of threat to the president or vice presidents. Because not everyone can subordinate their egos, the choice of an assistant requires great care. The president who runs through too many too fast becomes known as the "smiling facade" and the "in-office monster." Choosing to live with an ineffective assistant, on the other hand, will significantly compromise your presidency. The assistant is the professional confidante, the only person on campus with whom the president does not have to dust things off before saying them. Assuming the assistant has no significant line responsibility, freed of specific administrative duties, he or she will have a gestalt view of the institution, and be able to respond more in keeping with the president's interests. The loyal, intelligent, and broadly educated assistant who works fifteen hours a day and has enough sense to keep quiet, means an exceedingly fortunate president.

With a good assistant, the president can relax, blow off steam without fear of harsh judgment, discuss plans and strategies without obligation—even raise hell and still be considered a nice person.

The assistant and the secretary, if they are good, are the only persons on campus who really know the president, and must truly like and respect you just to put up with you.

The number of presidential assistants should depend on the size of the institution, the nature of the president, and the winds of the day. Often it is wise to designate a temporary special assistant for certain campus priorities like desegregation, affirmative action, retooling, budget/planning, and so forth.

Delegation

The conventional divisions are usually academic affairs, advancement (often called development or college/university relations), business affairs, and student services. Larger universities will often establish professional divisions, like medicine, and other areas such as alumni or government relations as line divisions reporting directly to the president. I rank advancement or development second because of the importance to a successful presidency of generating support and resources.

Some private colleges and universities, in particular, are placing increased emphasis on the cultivation of consumers and potential benefactors, even going so far as to create vice presidents for marketing. Regardless of the office to which this function is specifically assigned, the consumer orientation should be an important consideration within each line division of the institution.

Assuming the extraordinary competence of the top line officers, it is important that virtually all responsibilities for operating the institution can be delegated to them. While there should be overlapping, there should be no dual responsibilities. Under these conditions, the president can hold prime delegates accountable and still keep a finger in each area. Rarely should the president be involved in the direct operation of an office or department assigned to an officer of vice-presidential rank except in a convivial or observational manner. To touch base briefly with offices such as admissions, security, alumni, physical plant, and the academic departments is good for quality control and morale, and helps keep vice presidents honest. Deeper involvement would compromise the line of delegated vice-presidential authority and accountability. If a president chooses to become directly involved in an office, such as admissions, that ordinarily reports to a vice president, it is preferable to reorganize the office to report directly to the president rather than to risk the entire organization for a presidential preoccupation.

Some college presidents have reported that during periods of campus difficulty, their strongest, most unquestioning backers were support staff: secretarial, housekeeping, and maintenance people. This demonstrates how valuable those informal campus visits to touch base with people are.

The President's Executive Council

Weekly meetings of the key officers of the institution are a necessity that, with thought and care, can become a strong plus for the president. A fancy title—Executive Committee, President's Council, or Administrative Committee—helps. The members of this group will be the only people on campus who really know the president, besides a presidential assistant and secretary, but even here familiarity is to be guarded against. Katz (1973) concluded that "intimacy destroys illusions," and literally dozens of other studies support the concept of maintaining distance between a leader and staff (Stogdill, 1974). Vice presidents are the ultimate challenge because once there is little mystery left, the president is open and vulnerable. As was suggested earlier, to keep vice presidents in line and inspired is probably the greatest single presidential test. Good ones are like colonels wanting to be generals; when the general's stars are tarnished by familiarity, the distance doesn't seem so far.

Meetings of the executive group should be chaired by the president and include *only* the top line officers of the institution. There is no rational justification for regularly including in these meetings people who report to the top line officers, with the exception of a presidential assistant who takes notes and does not participate in the discussions unless invited to do so by the president. On some campuses, presidents include in their advisory group persons like the director of admissions or deans who report to vice presidents. Such officers should only make reports to the president's group and never be full-fledged members. To do otherwise clouds lines of responsibility and reduces the president's right to hold prime delegates accountable. The same is true for faculty and student representatives. Because they simply cannot be held accountable, they should not be included on a regular basis, regardless of pressure.

For purposes of communication and trust, the minutes of these meetings may be made public or at least available in a public place on campus, such as the library. If possible, let sufficient time pass before the minutes are published for any controversial content to dissipate. Usually, interested faculty are satisfied if the minutes are on record and available. In time, they will scarcely ever be read. But minutes should not be kept sacrosanct, for that creates an aura of secrecy that is unnecessary and counterproductive.

A frequent problem in presidential meetings is the "we" syndrome. Vice presidents, especially good ones, are at least subconsciously inclined to diminish or erode the authority, and reduce through increased intimacy the charisma of the president. It is here, out of sight of the community, that this tendency can be nipped in the bud. If it is not, the offending vice president will continue the behavior outside presidential meetings with faculty, other staff, students, and even trustees, and it will not be the fault of the vice president but of the president who allowed the behavior to pass in the first place. Although it is uncomfortable to say, each time a vice president refers to something "we" decided, he or she should be reminded decisively that "we" don't decide anything. This usually inhibits further attempts, unconscious or otherwise. This need not imply any lack of respect for your chief aides; rather, it serves as a healthy reminder to all, including the president, that after all is said and most is delegated, there still remains only one ultimately responsible officer—the president. Obviously, under these conditions, the vice presidents and the president have to be bound together by affection and respect as well as professional commitment. Nor does this suggest an imperial presidency; on the contrary, implemented early in one's administration, it insures against having to resort to imperiousness later when things may get out of hand.

The Chief Academic Officer

In spite of what has been said about the vice presidents being equal, the president's single most important professional associate is the chief academic officer, the prime conduit to the faculty and the president's de facto number two officer. No associate is more important, so despite the impact of democratization on the selection process, the president's must be the most significant role in the appointment. Extraordinary competence and complete loyalty are of fundamental importance, and a search committee process must not compromise either of these conditions. A mistake here can mean the president's undoing, for either his or her leadership will be eroded by an overly self-serving number two, or an inordinate amount of time will be spent in the academic area because the chief academic officer is incompetent.

If complete rapport with the president is a given, the prime personal ability of the chief academic officer is leadership through consensus building, a remarkable and rare skill. The academic chief should understand and support the president's vision and goals and be able to resolve issues effectively in a way that supports these. In most instances, this should happen without the president's involvement. Academic disagreements should never be personalized or they will remain barriers long after the issues have been resolved. The dean—or provost or vice president of academic affairs—who can be these things is rare; the president should look carefully into the background of all candidates to be sure of his or her mode of problem solving before making a final selection.

To find the academic officer, it is usually institutional policy to set up a broad-based selection committee (better called "advisory"). A committee member appointed by the president, usually the most valued assistant, should serve as administrator and handle correspondence and other details. The president must be certain that the committee has in the pool at least some candidates whom he or she generally endorses, and that after their deliberations, they recommend, not in rank order, from three to five acceptable candidates. If, after carefully evaluating each of these candidates, the president does not feel right about any, the committee should start over. Get a chief academic officer who has both your support and the support of the faculty representatives. The president who, to satisfy the immediate desire to get on with business, appoints a vice president for academic affairs about whom he or she has even the slightest reservations will regret it later. For although the faculty understandably want an important role in selection and will take all the authority granted them, they will still hold the president absolutely responsible for the officer's effective performance.

If you inherit a chief academic officer, assess the incumbent carefully and confer candidly with him or her about expectations. Because an incumbent seems to enjoy the respect of the faculty and a reputation for integrity does not mean that he or she will be a comfortable and loyal officer for any president. Academic deans serve at the pleasure of the president and should not hold tenure as administrators. If everything seems satisfactory about the incumbent, continuation in office should be confirmed but keep a watchful eye. Even the slightest variation from mutually understood expectations should be noted. A better sense of things should develop within a very few months. But most particularly, because of the importance of this vice president, do not let a nagging doubt go undiscussed because of embarrassment or uncertainty.

If the incumbent should go, the new president's predecessor should, if possible, ease the person out before the change in administration and appoint an acting chief academic officer until the new president can make a permanent selection. In this instance, a distinguished professorship with appropriate perks may be worth many times the price when weighed against a questionable chief academic officer or a popular one discharged by a new "axe-wielding" president. A board of trustees can be very helpful in this process, as long as it does not directly involve itself in the administration of the institution.

The wise and fortunate president has no closer relationship on campus than with the chief academic officer, sustaining, to the extent possible, the appropriate distance. (I should record here that I did not maintain this distance well during my presidency, but the chief academic officer was so able and good that there was never a problem.) The high degree of mutual respect between the two should be widely known by everyone, including other top administrators. With the right academic officer, the chances for a significant administration increase markedly.

In sum, administrators are the president's prime instruments, and should join with their leader in achieving the institutional vision as he or she has defined it. If they are superior, loyal, and enthusiastic, the president is well on the way to a successful tenure in office. And if you are able to inspire the trust and confidence of such superior persons, yours will be a grand experience and a good and perhaps distinguished presidency. Always remember that the president is expected to be the leader. Know that this is especially difficult to do during times of difficulty when there is temptation to blame faculty, students, trustees, and even your administrative colleagues. If you can survive the stress of hard times without faulting others, you will be "their president."

* Without truth and beauty, there is no university.

* Administrative subordinates either agree with the president, change the president's mind, or resign.

* Never violate the chain of command, but let associates know that you can.

* Surround yourself with superior persons, or you're dead.

* Loyalty is as important as ability; hire both.

* Rarely entertain vice presidents and their spouses.

* Be sure that you and your associates love one another. If not, they won't stand you for long.

* Leadership is five percent position and ninety-five percent mystique.

* The more committee meetings you attend, the less effective you are.

* On campus, let somebody else do it.

* Delegate everything but final authority.

* Don't retain or appoint an executive vice president unless you're on your last legs and still want to stay a few more years.

* Send flowers at least once a year to every secretary on the campus. They will repay you tenfold.

* You will never solve the parking problem. Delegate it to a committee and let it take the heat.

* Play around in office, but not that way.

* Unless invited, stay out of the personal lives of staff.

* Of course you're great, exceptional, and often persecuted, but you're also lucky to have your job.

CHAPTER 6

The President and Institutional Governance

Speak softly and carry a big stick. You will go far.
Theodore Roosevelt

OVER THE COURSE of the past twenty years, faculty members, students, and administrative staff have assumed increasingly larger roles in campus governance. The concept of shared governance, born at our leading institutions, has become well established at many colleges and universities and, properly exercised, can greatly facilitate your presidential power, particularly legitimate, expert, and charismatic power.

Retaining Final Authority

While faculties and students should participate in governance, their involvement should not give the impression of final authority over any dimension of the institution. Such arrangements lessen the ability of the president to lead and the institution to act, and defeat the very purpose of participation in the governance process. These nebulous arrangements serve neither faculty nor president, nor for that matter, students, trustees, and alumni; and divided authority simply does not meet the tests of troubled times. In virtually all dimensions of power, the arrangement lessens the possibility of effective leadership. The wise new president of an institution with such a system will immediately create an appointed or elected commission to study governance.

Ideally, a campus governance body has recommending authority over all matters that relate directly to the academic program and staff. Except for tradition and presidential uncertainty, there is no justification for giving such groups binding authority over any area or concern of the university, including the curriculum. In all matters, the president should be the authority who is ultimately accountable to both the trustees and the concerned public. Handled sensitively, this design greatly facilitates the opportunity for charismatic leadership as well as for leadership using each of the other forms of power.

The literature of leadership and power indicates that the best form of campus governance has three main ingredients. Those affected by decisions—faculty and students, but *not* administrative staff—should have a voice in their making. Administrators should be ex-officio nonvoting members. And lastly, the president must have final authority. Administrative staff are, in effect, agents of the president.

The Power of the President

The relationship of the president to the assembly is vitally important and mainly based on the extent to which the president is perceived on campus as having the status and authority to grant the privilege of participation in decision making. On campuses where that privilege is granted by trustees, state legislators, or, as is increasingly the case today, off-campus chancellors, the effectiveness of the president is significantly undermined. In terms of maximizing presidential effectiveness, all formal access to a governing board should be through the president.

Particularly in the public sector, statewide and multischool systems, coupled with the inhibitions of sunshine laws and required public meetings, often result in direct communication between presidential constituents (faculty, students, and administrative staff) and trustees and system officers, significantly reducing presidential power. Many systems become more impersonal; faculty members are attracted to unions and collective bargaining and dichotomies develop that make effective leadership less possible. The extent to which authority is vested in the office of the president and then delegated or granted by the president is undoubtedly the extent to which the president can be most effective.

I have served as a board member of six private colleges, and invariably, those institutions that have had the most problems and the highest presidential turnover are those whose members of the board have worked together with members of the college community (faculty, students, and most staff)—members who normally are expected to fall under the authority of the board's appointed president. Those campuses whose trustees establish faculty or student membership on board committees or directly invite faculty or student input or who assign trustees to interrogate members of the community (all in the name of effective communication and a concerned board, of course) are almost always in a state of nonproductive tension. It is the job of the president to stay in touch with the pulse of the campus constituency; if he or she isn't in touch, the board will find out about it soon enough.

The Use of the Presidential Veto and Influencing the Assembly

If the elected campus governance body only recommends, an effective relationship requires that the president rarely veto a recommendation from the assembly. The president who feels bound to use the veto often should probably make plans to move on, for it is obvious that there is little harmony between the leader and the campus. If such a poor relationship continues over an extended period, the president's charismatic power will be almost completely diminished.

But if the president and administrators play their roles effectively, vetoes will rarely be necessary. In assemblies within which high-ranking administrators participate in an ex-officio capacity, even without a veto, it is completely legitimate and ethical for them to attempt to influence the assembly's consideration of issues, whether in or out of session, but particularly the latter. The reader will recall that studies have found that people expect their leaders to influence them and are disappointed when they do not (Torrance, 1959, 1961; Torrance and Mason, 1956). Faculty, staff members, and students will find an administration united together in good spirit a legitimate and admirable force. Most negotiations should be conducted by the president's agents (administrators), and it is always preferable to have the votes going in.

Generally, faculty members like this system—except perhaps when it is explained this way—because their opinion, and that of a smaller but valuable student representation, is presented in an undiluted state to the president (through an appropriate dean or vice president, of course). Because presidential vetoes are rare, the process is accurately viewed by the campus community as the optimum in faculty-student participation in decision making. They not only participate but, in most instances, have the prime voice in academic decision making, yet the president both influences the voting process and remains in charge. This arrangement productively harnesses the talents of faculty and students, and, to most, is an acceptable form of shared governance.

A prudent president—in the spirit of Alexander Hamilton and the Whiskey Rebellion—may exercise the veto early in his or her term on a legitimate issue of comparative insignificance in order to demonstrate to the community that he or she has the authority and the will to use it. But with the exception of such ethical contrivances, the veto is a sign of failure.

Addressing the Assembly

There are other guidelines for presidential behavior vis-à-vis assemblies. Don't attend all assembly meetings, and when you do go, rarely stay for an entire meeting. The *first* item on the assembly agenda should be the president's report on campus activities and conditions, followed by questions. The president should not chair the assembly; the assembly should elect its own chair, usually a faculty member who meets with the president occasionally and the academic vice president regularly. This protects the president from accusations of unfairly trying to control the assembly while allowing dissent about both the system and issues to be registered. (Take no more heat than necessary.) At the one-on-one meetings with the assembly's elected chair, it is advisable to consult with the chair about important presidential decisions that could have campuswide reverberations, and to discuss things in general and become friends.

The president not only should *not* preside over the assembly, he or she should not even sit in the area designated for members. It is more effective, after an invitation to speak from the elected faculty chair, to rise from the gallery. Presidential remarks should usually reinforce the state-of-the-college/university address given in the fall at the opening faculty meeting (also attended by all administrators). Candidly inform the assembly about off-campus activities, including problems and strategies as well as successes. Speaking to the assembly openly and in depth implies confidentiality and trust and keeps the audience's interest. If a president does this well, neither faculty member nor student will ever violate the trust, and the charismatic ripples will extend throughout the community (trust and confidence).

Final Authority in More Complex Institutions

Some institutions, particularly among the largest, have multicameral campus-governance bodies, typically featuring separate organizations for students and faculty that independently make recommendations to the president. Other campuses have gone so far as to have tricameral systems, for faculty, students, and administrative staff respectively, each of which makes recommendations to the president. A few institutions even break these groups further down into subgroups. If possible, a president in this situation should try to bring representatives of these groups together in one unified body to reduce conflicting recommendations, but should not attempt to do away with the groups themselves.

Obviously, the key word here is *recommendation*. Regardless of how many formal groups exist on a campus, they must all make recommendations to the president. Although such systems diminish campus unity and ignore political realities, there are certain advantages for the president: his or her power can be even greater because of the fragmentation of campus opinion. In effect, the president becomes a broker, adjusting one faction's position to compromise with another and attempting to integrate all into the president's objectives. If ever forced to play one group against the other, the president should do so gently. Nonetheless, although the literature is not specific on this subject, a single unicameral campus-governance body is probably to the president's advantage, as well as serving the special interests of the several campus constituencies.

Collective Bargaining

At an institution with mandated collective bargaining, non-academic staff representation, or inappropriate trustee involvement in campus governance, the new president should either be assertive on the subject shortly after assuming office, or attempt to make the best of a bad situation by gingerly applying the tested concepts of power. (The presidential honeymoon is a time to accomplish wonders.) Sitting on such problems will not make them go away, but worsen.

With collective bargaining, although you should know and attempt to establish warm, personal relationships with union leadership, you should not discuss the specifics of working conditions with them. And when the time comes to negotiate, always send in an experienced negotiator and do not go yourself. (In most instances of collective bargaining, you won't even have the opportunity.) But collective bargaining need not be a bad thing so long as you respect its nature as being different from the more traditional patterns of shared governance. Don't make the mistake of thinking you are still colleagues in all things, but neither should you assume a harsh adversarial role. You are two distinct groups (management and employees) pursuing essentially the same goals from a different perspective. But if you don't have collective bargaining in your institution, in terms of your charismatic leadership potential, you are best advised to attempt to design a system (usually salary and personal perquisites) that is sufficiently attractive to staff that they will not find faculty unions attractive.

The campus-governance machinery can harness the collective intelligence of the campus community to common advantage, and also can serve as an effective channel through which the president inspires confidence, trust, and support. Only when they are viewed as adversaries will these groups become adversarial and a source of woe rather than benefit. Be patient, complete in your presentations, open in your answers, genuine in your respect for faculty-student representatives, unified in your administration, and spare in your attendance—and you will be rewarded beyond your expectations.

* Never allow any group on the campus to make final decisions; everything must be recommended to the president.

* Be brilliant, but failing that, shut up.

* Learn to lose, but don't like it.

* Rarely engage in give-and-take discussions on campus. You no longer enjoy the luxury of taking a chance on spontaneous brilliance or foolishness.

* Don't play your cards for pennies in petty displays of presidential authority.

★ Never compromise the fundamental neutrality of the university; the university cannot be temporarily irrational and maintain the respect of society. It is our collective irrationality during the past that is at the heart of our problems today.

CHAPTER 7

The President and the Faculty

The possession of unlimited power will make a despot of almost any person. There is a possible Nero in the gentlest human creature that walks.

Thomas Bailey Aldrich, 1903

FACULTY MEMBERS are the body and the heart of a college or university. It is they who must deliver, and they who are the most measurable test of a president's leadership, influence, and mission. Faculty members must be autonomous in their disciplines, respected in their governance role, and gently reminded from time to time that the final authority is the president. The president must lead, remind, and inspire the faculty beyond themselves. Concerning the presidential role vis-à-vis the faculty, it may be well to recall the daily adage used by the former vice chancellor of Cambridge University, Sir Eric Ashby, "I am a necessary evil."

The degree to which the president is respected and admired by the faculty will be the extent to which he or she is able to inspire trust and confidence, the extent to which he or she is believable and can deliver (in relative terms). To detail carefully for faculty the understandable reasons for your failure may be communication, but it certainly isn't effective and will only diminish your charismatic and expert potential.

Faculty members are frustrating, fretful, cynical, and critical, but also supportive, brilliant, and even magnificent. Only they can transform the president's vision into reality. They must be cajoled, challenged, and at times faulted, but most of

101

all, respected and appropriately included in all important decisions affecting the institution. One of the most pleasing events during my years in the presidency occurred when the president of the faculty association entitled his annual address to the trustees, "No Secrets." (This address was at the trustees' invitation; and ordinarily, such entrée to the trustees should not be encouraged.)

Faculty Leaders

Many faculties meet exclusive of the primary campus-governance body. In such cases, to make the elected leader of the faculty a voting member of the assembly is a valuable practice for both parties. It allows a faculty check on the assembly, and permits the administration to dilute the impact of negative faculty positions by providing a second chance to influence the deliberative process before resorting to a presidential veto.

The president or chair of the faculty should be viewed by the institution's president as the primary conduit for faculty opinion. Regular and frequent meetings with this person and serious efforts to cultivate his or her trust and friendship are in order. Here again, as is the case with the elected head of the campus-governance body, consultation prior to important decisions is vital. Prior discussion not only helps reach decisions, but also obliges the faculty leader not to bail out should problems develop after the presidential course is set.

However, other contacts with faculty are essential to establish and maintain presidential charisma. These less formal activities can help a president avoid a situation where so many voices speak for the institution that none does so effectively. Those frequent contacts with faculty convey to their elected leaders that you have other conduits to faculty opinion. Once again, the sensitive balance between distance and familiarity is an issue. There are ways to measure the pulse of the faculty accurately and, at the same time, to spare the president from overly ambitious faculty leaders who purport to speak for the faculty as a whole.

Staying in Touch with Faculty

There are many valuable techniques for staying in touch with faculty opinion without having to be exclusively dependent on the positions of elected faculty representatives. Staying in touch with the nonactivist, less political faculty members will provide valuable and often essential leverage in dealing with their elected spokespersons. Indeed, it will facilitate the president's being able to use effectively *all* of the forms of power discussed in Chapter 3.

Invitations to the president's office can be sent to randomly selected small groups of faculty regularly for "how's it going?" sessions (every six weeks or so). These informal gatherings should always begin with a statement from the president that reviews conditions, especially off campus, and includes a note of inspiration (the vision). After establishing a frame of reference in the opening remarks, invite questions and comments and treat them candidly. However, to insure an optimistic session, the president should both maintain center stage and be a good listener. Whenever else these meetings are scheduled during the year, they should always be held toward the beginning and end of the academic year. At the beginning of each year, faculty members and the president have more to be optimistic about; at the end, people can always look forward to the next fall. More of these sessions may be more important early in a presidency than later on, but they are always helpful.

The same kind of meeting—not under the auspices of the faculty, the assembly, or even the chief academic officer—should be scheduled for all new faculty (if you have any). These meetings should follow essentially the same format as above, but should especially emphasize the institution's mission and your presidential vision.

Frequent campus tours, at least weekly, provide an opportunity for everyone to see the president walking through classroom buildings. If invited, the president may even visit classes. Just stick your head in, wave, and see what happens. Regardless of the size of the campus, it is easy to identify all the coffee pots on the campus quickly. Dropping in on faculty members' offices for a brief conversation over coffee can also be exceedingly worthwhile. Make it a point to show up at least once a week where you are least expected.

Frequent and visible attendance at campus functions is important; this means getting used to feeling a bit obvious. At campus theater events and musical productions, mingle during intermissions, and go backstage afterwards to congratulate the performers. Every event should be viewed as a leadership role—an opportunity to foster trust and confidence.

Attendance at departmental social functions is not always a good idea, especially those for the president's own discipline; for there is a strong tendency to press overly hard on departmental affairs—so when you attend one, keep moving and try to avoid sit-down dinners. (There is no such thing as a purely social function for a president.) But never miss a retirement party, funeral, or memorial service; whenever possible under such conditions, accept an invitation to speak. These are rare opportunities to unify people as well as to express sincere appreciation or condolences. It's better to miss or be late for official meetings, even board meetings, than not to be present at a special occasion of great happiness or sorrow. It is also thoughtful to visit faculty, staff, and students who are confined in the hospital. They never forget, and you feel better about yourself.

Staying long at departmental or administrative parties is a mistake, and those presidents who are relaxed by liquor shouldn't drink. A good idea is always to imply that you have at least one more social function that evening than is actually the case. After a while, an experienced president can make remarks (if appropriate) and the rounds in twenty to forty-five minutes and be off. (Besides, people enjoy themselves more without the president; your absence gives them something to talk about.)

The president who plays bridge, chess, or better yet, poker, or who is a has-been athlete, can take the opportunity to play with faculty and staff. It's wise to mix on-campus and off-campus types, and in athletics like basketball, even students. These activities are great levelers that don't sacrifice position when done occasionally. They are better than most social events because everyone is too involved to pressure the president to talk business.

Faculty Meetings

Faculty meetings are not the best way to stay in touch with faculty opinion. Indeed, they can become so familial and leveling that the president is reduced to little more than a coordinator, and an ineffective one at that. In Chapter 4, the design of faculty meetings was discussed, but here it is appropriate to remind the reader that, although custom demands general meetings of the faculty on most campuses, they are of little value in terms of institutional direction, conflict resolution, or presidential leadership. If held too often (and two a year should be enough), they can do great damage to the effective conduct of the institution and your presidential vision; and all in the name of better communication. In terms of the five power forces, other than a faculty meeting in the fall at which you present a state-of-the-institution address and a charge for the year, and a second at midyear where the chief academic officer speaks, you should call general meetings of the faculty only during periods of emergency where you will be provided a charismatic opportunity. But to try to resolve a serious problem at a general faculty meeting will almost invariably result in an uneasy solution, if any, and a frustrated and less effective president.

Be the President with Faculty

As already suggested, presidents can scarcely afford the luxury of taking a chance on spontaneous brilliance and should arrange their presentations to the extent possible. For example, a president can offer seminars on subjects about which he or she feels comfortable and qualified, or write book reviews, but never review a book written by a member of the faculty. Occasionally, the president can attend campus seminars and ask penetrating questions, always avoiding irrelevant debate or controversy.

Other activities can enhance the president as a leader in the faculty's eyes. Whatever the activity, the president must remember that he or she is not "one of them" while occupying the presidential office, regardless of your past achievements in a discipline, or what they say. It is only natural for faculty to try to keep or make you one of them; but if they succeed, it will be your fault, and you will be less effective as their president.

Recent research on faculty attitudes and presidential styles indicates that of the four styles identified—bureaucratic, intellectual, egalitarian, and counselor—the one most directly associated with faculty insecurity and perceived presidential ineffectiveness is the intellectual president; and, interestingly, this is the president "who most frequently communicates with faculty" (Astin and Sherrei, 1980). It is also the intellectual president who experiences the most frustrations and disappointments with faculty and who is least "trusted" by fellow administrators. This is probably the president who should have stayed on the faculty in the first place, for he or she lacks the confidence and commitment to establish sufficient distance from the faculty to lead them. Nonetheless, David Riesman (1980) reported that faculty members serving on presidential search committees tend to select candidates for president who have the characteristics of someone they would most like to have as a colleague—an interesting set of contradictions.

Even more than administrative associates, faculty must be credited for successes, and you must assume responsibility for failures. Faculty support is fickle, never to be taken for granted. In commenting on the faculty, one administrative assistant recounted the following:

> I remember one state university president staring contemplatively out his window at a swarm of faculty coming out of an adjacent building following a general faculty meeting. "Look," he

said, "there go a couple thousand people who are convinced that they know more about how to run this university than I do." [Carbone, 1981]

Friendships between a president and a faculty member can result in the friend supporting the president in hard times but arguing about every substantive decision or course of action. Such friendships can erode leadership because good friends simply know each other too well for any of the power forces to be effectively used. For the president who has been appointed from within the institution, the best advice is to be as "presidential" as possible without violating your obligations to close friendships. Do your best not to discuss the institution and its problems with them. Bear in mind, when tempted to become too personal in your relationships, that strong leaders who can deliver results are more admired and supported than leaders who are more friendly and democratic but who, because of their egalitarian natures, cannot back up their friendly stance through effective action.

In sum, faculty are the heart of the institution; they can be both a presidential bane and a blessing. They should be granted the right to interpret their subjects as they will, subject, of course, to peer and student evaluation; but, in all other matters, their role should only involve recommending. It is important to stress again, however, that they should play a significant role in virtually all campus affairs. And if you conduct yourself wisely, you can be their leader, benefit from their insight, and enjoy their company. But always remember—you are the president.

* If you have close personal friends on the faculty (and you probably will), be careful.

* Teach now and then.

* Insist that the faculty know more about the affairs of the institution than they want to.

* To schedule more than two faculty meetings a year is an exercise in intellectual anarchy and will yield a thou-

sand directions, an unhappy faculty, and a frustrated president.

* Sometimes you will never know for certain.

* Listen to everyone, and seek out the quiet performers.

* The president who spends too much time in the faculty dining room remains or becomes a member of the faculty and should return there.

* The extent to which you are one of the boys (or girls) is the extent to which you are one of the boys (or girls).

* The value of your presidency will be the extent to which you maintain fidelity in individual relationships with faculty, students, associates, and all others.

* Always convert every complainer into a supporter, and try to do the same with your adversaries.

CHAPTER 8

The President and the Students

The first flush of power is done in caricature.
C. Richard Gillespie, 1970

THE BEST INTERESTS of each individual student should be the criterion against which the president evaluates virtually every decision. This tests presidential motives and heightens the trust and confidence placed in the office by the community.

You will have no greater opportunity for charisma than with students, for their good opinion will extend to all of your power objects. Yet, many presidents take little time for students, probably because of anxiety that is rationalized as more pressing concerns. Students, along with support staff, can be the most enthusiastic, courageous, and valuable source of presidential support, for students will go right down to the wire with a president whom they admire.

Students are idealistic, bold, uninhibited, and, unlike many of their mentors, not too sophisticated to give open admiration and affection, but these must be earned. It is important to try to gain student support early in an administration, because initial impressions are so significant, for they carry on from generation to generation, and after students become alumni, they will remember even more warmly.

109

Activities with Students

Surveys consistently indicate that students would like to see more of their presidents (ACE-UCLA Freshman National Astin, 1981). There are no student activities, roles, or moods unimportant to a president. Starting with the orientation program for new students, be present whenever possible. Use a color videotape for orientation programs when you can't attend. In time, you may find that the videotape is an excellent substitute; the association with television and movies inspires an extraordinary sense of presidential importance.

Presidential talks to new students should be inspirational and elevating, and the larger the group the better, although one-on-one sessions with students are also important. Academic regalia at a fall orientation or convocation, like other campus ceremonies, can contribute to the aura of leadership. It sets the mood for the year, and that mood could be important by the following spring.

The astute president knows that an hour in the residence halls in September is worth literally weeks the next spring when trouble may strike. During the period that students are moving into the halls, show up for a part of each day to welcome parents and students informally, from time to time help carry luggage or boxes, or just sit on the curb in front of a freshman residence unit and visit. Here again, the key is not to get off the presidential platform. (Don't carry luggage all day; just show the people that you're not so impressed with yourself that you can't carry luggage.) Parents as well as students and staff never forget these gestures, and they will give you more credibility during periods of difficulty than a spate of presidential proclamations.

Residence halls are best considered the students' home. With few exceptions (the bull sessions), only go there when invited. Invitations can come from individual students as well as from residence-hall leaders and councils. Indeed, the popcorn and Pepsi sessions where the president sits on the floor with a group of students at 11:30 at night are usually the best (except on your stomach).

At most community and commuter colleges and universities, spending time at the student union or center, the book store, or registration serves the same purpose. Most presidents will find a combination of residence hall and other campus social centers most valuable. (A good check on the registration program is to ask a cross section of students how long it took and what their impressions of registration were.)

Eating and drinking with students is a way to evaluate the quality and efficiency of the campus food service, to visit informally with students, and to increase your charisma. Take your food tray and go up and ask to join them; most will be delighted. You, of course, must take the initiative. One president wondered why he couldn't relate effectively to students. He said, "I even go out on the campus and sit on a bench, and nobody joins me."

Knowing the social centers of the campus and regularly making the rounds is also good leadership. Usually, a campus sociogram develops within the first few weeks of school; the straights, the jocks, the all-Americans, the blacks, the right, the left, the artists, and so on each congregate in certain locations, with the lovers and loners sprinkled around the edges. By knowing these locales, a president can take the pulse of the student community each morning before going to the office. If you regularly make the rounds, it is no surprise when you occasionally stop for coffee and a brief chat. It takes no more than ten to thirty minutes to visit most of the student nerve centers every morning and still be in the office by 8:30 or 9:00, regardless of the size of the campus. (Vary the time of day occasionally.)

Attend student dances, debates, theater, and sports events, and make drop-in appearances at residence-hall or student-union bull sessions. And be visible: If you are at a dance, *dance,* or at least try; if you are at a football or basketball game or at the theater, be seen and circulate. Visits to players and coaches in the locker room after losses are ill advised unless the team is particularly heartbroken. On the other hand, the president should always be around for victory celebrations. Whether made in defeat or in victory, the visit is best kept short.

Student Leaders

Characteristics of student leaders change with the times. During periods of relative campus tranquility, they are usually conservative, even inclined to refer to the president as "sir" or "ma'am." But during campus unrest, they are almost invariably more challenging. Every meeting with the president is a confrontation or, at least, they try to make it one. Often they will go to great lengths to avoid a one-on-one session with the president; for they also know, at least intuitively, that if the president closes the distance between them, they will risk compromising whatever their goals. If you can't get them alone on campus, pursue them to the lairs; they can usually be found there late at night.

Generally speaking, student body and class officers are more conservative, malleable, and less influential than student newspaper editors and experienced reporters. The leaders of Greek groups and other campus organizations are typically the most conservative and supportive of all. Obvious exceptions are radical and extremist organizations, especially troublesome during periods of unrest. During such periods, more traditional student leaders will want to help offset extremists. Use them. It is important, however, that the president know leaders of all important student groups, regardless of how fractious, and attempt to establish an honest rapport.

Rapport with the president of the student body and the editor of the campus newspaper is especially important and can be easily established, assuming commitment and sincerity on your part. Invite each to your office for a private session immediately after his or her election or appointment. (If possible, initiate private meetings with all the candidates for these key posts before the winners assume office—for it will provide links with virtually all activist or potential activist groups on campus.) Avoid forums where you are put on the spot by student leadership hopefuls; regardless of their brilliance, presidents always lose in such settings.

Assuming the student body president is elected in the late spring, it is often helpful to appoint the winner to a summer internship in the president's office. This can give the president an advantage when school starts in the fall because of the opportunity for rapport, and it also helps the new student body president understand the nature and procedures of a college or university.

In the fall, establish *weekly* private meetings with the student body president and the newspaper editor or their representatives; put these on the calendar and try always to be there. Talk about everything from your agenda to the student's personal plans. This kind of relationship almost invariably proves valuable for everyone, but especially during periods of difficulty.

Saying No

Although most bad news should be conveyed by deans and vice presidents, at times the president also has to say no to student leaders. A decisive no will be respected and usually adhered to, but should be explained in person rather than through messages or notes. Occasionally, there is a really poor student leader; if of limited influence, these are best ignored. But if such a student holds a key campus position, any dealings the president has should be candid and direct and not veiled with false acceptance. The student's impact can also be diminished by cultivating his or her associates—vice presidents, assistant editors, and the like. I once challenged such a student body president to debate in the University Union, hoping that he wouldn't accept. He didn't, and instead, resigned a short time later. I was relieved.

Other Ways to Influence Students and Their Leaders

Some of the best ways to insure presidential influence with student leaders, including those on the campus newspaper, are to hold regular and well-advertised student office hours each week, attend student social functions and stay a while, speak to student groups, and get out on the campus and be seen. One college president related that picking up student hitchhikers later saved the day for him more than once. Here again, the point is that by showing student leaders that they are not the president's only conduits to student attitude and opinion, their furor and even their influence can be greatly reduced. Students will be unusually inclined to work cooperatively with your administration, and rarely will they display a "we/you" attitude.

Generally, student leaders are motivated by the same things that motivate a president; they are just not as sophisticated. The great measure are good, decent, concerned persons with a sense of mission, anxious to advance their cause and themselves. Real zealots are rare, except in fringe groups, and caution has already been recommended in dealing with these people, whether they come from the right or left. But most student leaders will respect and like the president, given half a chance. They will listen, even change their positions, if you make sense, and line up right behind you when the chips are down. Respect is more important than friendship, for, contrary to conventional contemporary assumptions, a leader/follower relationship is still what students—and most other people—expect. The president who establishes genuine and close relationships with students will have a legion of supporters for life.

Student Unrest

From time to time during a president's tenure, it may be his or her unpleasant duty to deal with hostile student groups, which often contain a sprinkling of faculty and off-campus hangers-on. The best policy in such situations is to send the appropriate vice president, usually the student personnel officer, who can use the experience. Too many presidents feel that they have something to prove and go into these situations without regard for the chain of delegated responsibility. One of the surest ways to lose whatever presidential mystique you have is to louse up during a student confrontation. Remember, the key to an effective presidency is presidential charisma, and charisma is best fostered in structured situations.

But if there is an occasion where your reputation has been placed on the line, you may feel bound to meet a group of hostile protestors. In such a situation, if at all possible, the group should come to the president's territory, preferably in or near the administration building. It should be a public place, a corridor or lounge, not the president's office. (If students forcefully occupy that office or anywhere else on campus, they should be *carefully* arrested after being so advised and given a reasonable amount of time to vacate the premises.) The president should meet the group alone, without a protective entourage of staff and associates; invariably this will take them off guard. It is wise to have trusted associates scattered throughout a hostile crowd, but they should not participate in the dialogue. In such settings, with your supporting structure virtually gone, it is best to divest yourself completely of your presidential appointments; it will not only disarm the protestors but it will allow you a better opportunity to establish a "charismatic moment."

Always try to confront the full body of protestors rather than agree to meet with representatives of a protesting faction. Because a college president is likely to have more experience making presentations to a group than student leaders, this gives the president an advantage. It also allows the president to spot opportunities to divide the group and get factions debating one another. By contrast, meeting with representatives allows the president's adversaries to present themselves as legitimate opponents, and to interpret even a written presidential message as they will. Resist the temptation to meet with what, at the moment, may appear to be a smaller and therefore less threatening group.

If possible, obtain the group's demands in advance of the meeting. This gives you the advantage of speaking first and tends to diffuse the group's solidarity behind its goals. Any president should absolutely refuse to respond to nonnegotiable demands, without casting judgments as to their intrinsic legitimacy.

Speak extemporaneously or from notes, but do not use a prepared text. If possible, the session should be unobtrusively taped. Prepare a press release before the session to be quickly edited afterwards. Speak for at least ten minutes, calling as many students by name as possible. Explaining the president's role and responsibility, lead with remarks that draw you together with the group and only then address their demands. In most cases, a president will be able to evade actually answering the demands by pledging to present in writing reactions within a mutually agreeable time period. The president who can do this may be able to end the session as a hero and dissipate the group's hostile energies at the same time. If the leaders haven't read or remembered Sol Alinsky's *Rules for Radicals* (1972), the president is home free, at least for the moment.

Insist on civility throughout your remarks. Questions should be invited after the president speaks but neither long speeches nor attempts to cut short answers should be tolerated. (If interrupted, keep talking.)

Accepting a little abuse is actually not a bad idea. Some members of protesting groups may hurl names, be rude, or say things that would ordinarily prompt a strong response. Don't overreact to this behavior; you can actually gain support from otherwise unsympathetic members of the audience.

After a reasonable period, no more than an hour, simply thank the group for their attention and leave. When leaving, be joined by an associate or two to prevent the possibility of continued discussion during the departure. The idea is to keep the entire session under your control, not theirs.

After the confrontation, encourage members of the group to talk individually; most of them feel guilty. Some may even tearfully come to the president's office to apologize. Regardless, if you spot them alone or in small groups on campus, talk to them. Other administrators cannot do this in place of the president. The aftermath of confrontation is an ideal time to build strong relationships and inspire understanding and support.

Finally, don't hold a grudge, regardless of what has been said or done. Within the bounds of ethics, enlisting members of dissident groups can produce valuable allies for the future. Their presence during meetings brewing radical causes can often prevent problems. One president hired as his assistant the student leader who spoke most vigorously against him during a campus strike; that student is now a college vice president. Another president finally won over a student who had once declared the president an "incarnate evil." Since that time, the student has become a prominent journalist and has written more than a half-dozen flattering personality profiles of the president in major local and regional publications.

Chief Student-Services Officer

Another critical communication link to students is the chief student-services officer, the president's in-house superego, a conscience against which to weigh decisions affecting students. The longer a president's tenure in office, the more likely he or she is to take for granted or forget the primary importance of students. So, regardless of the president's background, a highly placed person in the administration should be charged with student advocacy.

The role of a professional student advocate is too important to be delegated to just another manager. Loyalty and competence are of course important, but the person must be able to speak effectively for students and accurately assess their moods. "Company" types don't work well in this position. Such a person is willing to argue with a president yet is steadfastly loyal whatever position is decided upon. Within the terms of loyalty, the chief student-services officer must be free to advocate; and, during periods of difficulty, his or her position may be in conflict with the advice you get from your other vice presidents. Remember personal chemistry in this appointment, for you may often hear things from your chief student advisor you'd rather not hear. Listen thoughtfully, and then strike your own course.

Although a questionable practice perhaps, student services, student affairs, or student personnel areas have grown significantly during recent years. They often include such areas as counseling, remedial programs, residence halls and off-campus housing, student unions, student organizations, and often admissions, financial aid, health centers, and athletics. Although I personally question this plethora of responsibilities, for it tends to make administrators out of student-services officers who ought to be advocates, if you have such an arrangement, or a similar one, your chief student-services officer must also be a capable manager who understands fully the principles and practice of delegation and accountability. To find a person who combines the attributes of student advocate and manager is difficult; but, under such conditions, you must—for, if you appoint only an advocate, you have a constant administrative mess; and if you appoint the manager, you find yourself unadvised or ill-advised about students during periods of difficulty.

Faculty are the body of the university, but students are its lifeblood; a good and successful president recognizes this, honestly cultivating them, understanding them, striving to earn their respect and affection, and never taking them for granted. After you have left office, there will be few things that make you feel better than a former student who meets you and warmly says, "We miss you."

* An hour in the residence halls in September is worth a week in April.

* Test your convictions on each new student generation. In the process you will change and stay honest.

* Never act out of uncontrolled anger; be ashamed when you do.

* Make decisions based on the best interests of the individual student, not the department, the institution, the state, or the church—or even the pressing demands of student politicians.

* Never countenance the violation of the duly constituted law.

* Play basketball with students. It's humbling.

* Don't be afraid of group confrontations. They can be fruitful and exhilarating, but always go into them alone.

* Try to be out of the office and on campus during the first week and last week of school; you can be gone the rest of the time and not be missed.

* When students start calling you by your first name, you probably need a haircut.

* If you want an irresponsible student generation, grant them amnesty when they violate the law.

* Never agree to consider nonnegotiable demands.

* Once when I was being confronted by a group of hostile protest marchers, two businessmen who had been visiting our placement office were overheard remarking about their great admiration for me under such difficult conditions. One of the protest marchers heard the conversation and said, "What the hell do you think they pay the bastard for?"

* Dance with students. It's fun.

CHAPTER 9

Power Off Campus: The President and Persons of Influence

Anyone who isn't heard outside the campus isn't worth being heard inside.

Father Theodore M. Hesburgh

God is usually on the side of the big squadrons against the little ones.

Roger DeBussy Rebutin, 1667

Always do right. This will gratify some people, and astonish the rest.

Mark Twain, 1901

To BECOME INFLUENTIAL, a president must be visible. To become visible, the president must be bold, which demands risking being controversial. To remain at all comfortable and retain the presidency under such conditions, it is essential to know what you're talking about. That requires reading, listening, and, above all, surrounding yourself with superior persons. To keep superior persons, a president must take care of them and be exciting. Being exciting means being visible and bold. And so it goes.

The president is the primary factor in the activity that will insure the success of off-campus ventures—the cultivation, enlistment, and involvement of external constituencies. Recent books on presidential style and leadership effectiveness pay less attention to external affairs than to any other relevant

121

topic (Astin and Scherrei, 1980; Benezet et al., 1981). No responsibility is more important to presidential success (Fisher, 1980); yet many presidents rationalize by saying that they are bogged down with more important matters on campus or that they are just plain uncomfortable dealing with off-campus people and conditions; and, with the exception of the role of governments, scholars of the presidency rarely write about external affairs.

The "Intellectual" President

Presidents who have arrived at the presidency through the academic chairs are especially prone to shun their external responsibilities. Indeed, many presidents of this type never quite make it onto the presidential platform because they are unable to draw sufficiently far away from their academic background where they are more comfortable (Astin and Scherrei, 1980). Yet it is the "intellectual" president who not only seems to do poorly with his or her external constituency but who also has the most serious problems with faculty and staff. Academics are often cynical, and sometimes condescending and patronizing in their attitudes toward nonacademic types. An individual at all inclined this way, thrust into the "outside world" as a solicitor, may well find an unsettling experience. But despite these feelings and the dearth of material on the subject, no aspect of a presidency is more important than activities with external constituencies. Anyone who is only comfortable in the faculty dining room should return to the faculty before doing untold damage to the college or university.

Institutional Advancement: The President's External Affairs Arm

Most colleges and universities have a line division called development, public affairs, or institutional advancement—or some combination of these. It usually includes professionals in public relations, fund raising, alumni relations, publications, and government relations who can help a president relate to external groups. This division should rank just behind the academic affairs division in terms of fiscal priorities. These two divisions are the basic determinants of the charismatic president's administration. Indeed, the degree to which a president is able to use wisely the professionals in institutional advancement may well represent the difference between the presidency being bland, colorless, and undistinguished or exciting, significant, and stimulating. The president, however, is the key player in the external affairs program.

External affairs officers can be a president's greatest asset in the quest to enhance charismatic influence systematically; treat them as such. Like all functionaries, including presidents, advancement professionals can sometimes lose sight of the goal in a forest of unrelated particulars, and may need reminding.

A president simply must be able smoothly and effectively to negotiate the external forces that will determine the future of the institution. To take these for granted or assume that someone else will or can completely handle this role for a president is complete folly. The following chapters will consider the rationale, systems, and techniques of external relations in greater detail. These chapters concentrate on how to use the various forms of presidential power with each of the following external groups: influential persons and benefactors, trustees, politicians, public figures and bureaucrats, the media, and alumni. It should also be said here that complete information on each aspect of administering an institutional advancement program is available from the Council for Advancement and Support of Education (CASE) in Washington, D.C.

The President and the General Principles of External Relations

There are some general principles to adhere to in all external relations. Here again, the charismatic characteristics of distance, style, and perceived self-confidence must be cultivated, for most presidents have little legitimate and reward power and almost no coercive power in external situations. The degree to which a president is able to establish charismatic qualities is, in large measure, the degree to which he or she is able to use expert power effectively and advance the institutional mission.

It will be wise to remember these points from Chapters 2 and 3 on research:

1. Too much informal behavior may reduce effectiveness; the president is always the president. Stay on the platform.

2. Although the president should be involved in many external activities and arenas, the involvement should not be too deep, for deep involvement risks virtually all of your power forms as well as exhausts an inordinate amount of time. Your first and primary obligation is to the institution; spread yourself around, be visible, be brief but genuine, and you will be charismatic.

3. The president's effort to influence external conditions to the advantage of the institution should not be equivocal. People in the external community expect and need to hear your vision as much as those on campus.

4. When speaking to groups, individuals, or the media, know the subject and try to be the only expert on it in the group. Ordinarily, presidential panels are to be avoided, especially on television.

5. Trappings are just as important to a presentation off campus as on.

6. A small entourage can be important with off-campus groups; at least take along an assistant. Make your solo appearances disarming, rather than the rule.

7. Speeches to an external audience should be delivered

from its perspective, not the president's. Once again, merit does not win out. (More on this later.)

8. It is important that those off campus *like* the president. Within the limits of your nature and code of ethics, try to be attentive to and interested in nonacademic types. In time you will like them.

9. The president must always at least appear energetic. Never tell a reporter, a trustee, or a politician that you are tired or harassed, and don't tell anyone that you have a cold or need sleep.

The Newly Appointed President

The first, essential order of business in external affairs for a newly appointed president is to begin immediately to seek and accept community speaking engagements that are important enough to be reported in the local media. Speak to everyone, from the American Legion to the World Federalists—the right and the left, social and service groups, political and professional organizations, religious and recreational groups. The larger the group is, the better. Appearances on radio and television and quotation in newspapers and magazines should be sought. (If given a choice between a newspaper feature and an article in a professional journal, always take the newspaper. Remember that your effectiveness will not be primarily determined by publication in distinguished academic journals.)

If possible, write regular features for local newspapers on any subject the papers are willing to print. Or do a regular radio or television show. Never turn down an opportunity to appear as a principal on a show or to be the subject of a feature article. An institutional leader who isn't a good public speaker or feels unusually uncomfortable on television, should talk to a public-relations professional about getting help. These public appearances should be candidly critiqued by the president's assistant and advancement staff, and their objective responses should not be confused with disloyalty.

Although debatable among public-relations professionals, it may be of value for your staff to issue news releases on all of your formal appearances. At this writing, a friend called with the happy news that he had just been appointed to his long-sought college presidency. After sharing the joy of the moment, he asked the awkward question, "Jim, should I write my own press release?" I responded unequivocally, "Yes," and reminded him that he was not going to Harvard and of the importance of those first presidential steps. I then advised him to have his draft release edited by the PR officer (whom he knows well) at his present institution and to have the PR officer send the release to his new PR office.

For the most part, institutional news releases are only picked up by small local or weekly papers, but these are useful; and occasionally major dailies may print an item. Releases should also be sent to television and radio stations, which sometimes pick up stories missed by the newspapers. They should also be sent to members of boards and others you influence. Invitations to appear at celebrity events and tournaments, even the "right" fashion shows, are best accepted. The aim is to become known and admired by the general public. Do not assume, however, that presidential advancement is the only dimension of college and university public relations—far from it; a good public-relations program includes media cultivation by staff, feature stories about campus programs, people, unusual scholarly and research activities, and other things.

In the course of time, presidents take chances, and upon occasion, become controversial. Whatever the controversy, it goes without saying that the cause must be worthy and the case sound and above logical contradiction. (Another reason why the president's associates must be superior is to be able to buttress presidential generalizations.)

With a good external relations program politicians will assume their constituents admire the president, bureaucrats will think that politicians do, trustees and influential persons will assume that everyone does, and the media will find you interesting. What the president must never forget is that this image is largely undeserved and must regularly be reviewed, re-fueled, and refined by more objective advisors. Pity the pres-ident who takes his image to heart; but have one you will, so shape it as carefully as possible.

You Are the Star

With rare exceptions (Princeton, Stanford, et al.), the pres-ident, rather than the institution, must be the star. While there will be others who receive major public recognition, none must, for long, exceed the president's; for it is the president who must lead, and publicity fuels your charismatic image and your ability to lead.

While president, do not expect to speak to anyone on nonpresidential terms. Presidents learn to cherish the rare an-onymity they find, and become ever more grateful for the friends they have. As I learned in Greece a few years ago, there are few things more disconcerting, when walking down a village lane singing with friends, beer in hand, than suddenly to meet a student from the university who says, "President Fisher, what a surprise seeing you here."

George Bernard Shaw said, "You get a man through his religion, not yours." Whether talking to a potential contribu-tor, reporter, trustee, Rotary Club, legislative committee, or alumni group, never be so thoughtless or so absorbed in con-veying your vision and message that you fail to appreciate the conditions that motivate the audience. Including in the presentation the listener's power centers, especially in the case of politicians, will almost invariably win your cause. The merit of a cause is never sufficient; it may win sympathy but rarely the day. A speaker who ignores the listeners' concerns is likely to become known as that "nice guy who is completely unrealistic," a person few treat seriously off campus—and, in time, on campus also. He or she is also the president who becomes bitter and hostile toward off-campus decision makers, and it's hard to hide those feelings.

The External Influence Power Hierarchy

To succeed in external relations, the president must identify and cultivate the people with the money and power to help the college or university reach its goals. With this important group, charismatic and expert power are in order, with a measure of legitimate and reward power and virtually no coercive power. This hierarchy of wealthy and influential people is more important than the governor, the education and editorial writers for the major newspaper, and in many instances, even the trustees. If a president can come to be viewed as one of the hierarchy, he or she will be able to command the admiring attention of all the others. For in spite of proclamations and protestations to the contrary, this hierarchy ranks at the top of the socioeconomic scale in all communities. They are corporate leaders, the newspaper publishers, and the wealthy landed families who are the local aristocracy. You have an advantage with these leaders, for they have more respect for a college or university president than politicians, most trustees, and the media typically have. They still derive a certain self-enhancement from being associated with you, and your presence with them is reassuring about the general order of things.

Once again, distance, style, and perceived self-confidence are crucial. Regardless of your own social background, do not be obsequious or obviously uncomfortable. Comport yourself with dignity and as much grace as possible without contrivance. The president who has already incorporated these charismatic leadership qualities into his or her style can just be him or herself. Failure to do so soon means being ignored, for your presence can become an uncomfortable embarrassment for them.

Who's Who

The president who did not come from the local aristocracy should have the advancement staff put together a book on the local hierarchy. Each entry should include as much as possible about each: photograph, education, assets, interests, persuasions, politics, family, and so forth. Absorb this to the extent that you rarely have the sense of meeting a person for the first time.

Although it is important to know "who pulls whose strings," don't be quite so candid in written materials. I once sent a quick, inquisitive, former student body president who had just graduated to the state capital in Illinois to do a profile on key members of the state legislature. When he returned from the first trip, his material included so much information about the personal lives of some important actors in the state that I quickly expunged the information and gave more explicit instructions for the next trip.

With this "Who's Who" prepared and learned, the president is ready to cultivate these people in nonstress, nonproblem settings. They should not be asked for anything specific until a relationship has developed. This means spending numerous evenings attending civic functions, serving on hospital and symphony boards, giving speeches, attending cultural and athletic activities, and spending precious but healthy hours on the tennis court or golf course. It's the after-activity conversations and drink breaks that pay off. Anyone uninterested or unable to do most of these things is probably the wrong person for the job.

Country Clubs and Service Clubs

Unless the setting is a small town, it is generally not a good idea to join either social or service clubs. Vice presidents and other administrators can belong to the Rotary and Kiwanis; the president speaks to them. Until invited, the president can let friends ask about membership in the most prestigious clubs. But after joining a club or other group, some of the advantages of distance are lost. Join only the very top organizations, if you join at all. Finally, although joining a country club may be a good idea, it can jeopardize credibility among some constituencies. Although there are notable exceptions, a president should rarely be publicly identified as a member of a group or even a political party. The president of an institution can best gain the support of those who count if he or she has few such encumbrances.

Appointments to Boards, Commissions, et al.

Appointment to community or statewide commissions, task forces, and the like can be of value. If the mayor, governor, or other public official extends such an invitation, it's usually because a president is achieving a significant public reputation, or, alternatively, because the official needs a respected public person to use as a buffer for a decision that may be unpopular. The president's staff should carefully research and critique all the possible consequences before responding, but if possible, these invitations should be accepted. For instance, it's a no-win situation if the governor's invitation is to serve on a commission to locate a new site for the state prison, but if you are the president of a public institution, the prospects are good if that commission's assignment is to increase legislators' salaries.

Getting the Hierarchy Involved on Campus

Although the reverberations of public activities and speeches will eventually result in invitations, a president shouldn't wait that long to begin cultivating the local hierarchy. One of the best ways to attract their interest is to elevate the cultural and athletic events sponsored by the institution. Arts balls and exhibits, special events, speakers and performances that appeal to the right people, and major tennis tournaments are possibilities. And several of these activities also generate additional revenues.

Meals are good situations within which to meet with members of the hierarchy. Luncheons are better than dinners, and breakfasts are best. For the most part, extend luncheon and breakfast invitations and accept dinner invitations. Until in office for a while, few presidents can induce many truly important people to come to dinner, and end up wasting valuable time and institutional money entertaining faculty, staff, and friends who can't help the institution much.

One on One is Best

By far, the best way to establish good relationships with others is one on one in informal and relaxed settings. Some prefer tennis and sailing, but golf and other recreational activities serve as well. The most efficient way I found to establish good and valuable personal relationships with important people was to hold breakfasts in the presidential boardroom. The guest was invited to come any time between 6:30 and 9:00 A.M. I prepared breakfast with the help of a good assistant who was out of sight by the time the guest arrived. I would seat the guest, pour coffee, and call his or her attention to reading materials beside the breakfast plate (the morning newspaper on the bottom of the pile, and my most important message on top). At the appropriate time, I served breakfast, and we would almost invariably proceed naturally to discuss the informal agenda set by the pile of materials the guest had looked through while I finished preparing the meal. They were impressed that I did the cooking, and it also cost less than having it prepared by staff. The person almost always came because few people extend breakfast invitations. Those persons with whom I had breakfast through the years became the institution's most constant supporters and contributors.

Dress

With this group, there is another sensitive subject to be addressed—dress. Local aristocracies everywhere are virtually the same in their interests, values, activities, and *clothing styles*—Brooks Brothers or clothing that looks like

Brooks Brothers. And they can spot kindred souls anywhere by their dress. Many college and university presidents look like they just stepped from the pages of an old and wrinkled Montgomery Ward or J.C. Penney catalog (it's not so bad if it's patched Harris Tweed); others foolishly try to affect the latest student styles. It is all right to economize, but a president ought to buy the right look. For men, this involves conservative (three-button), well-cut suits with appropriate shoes, ties, belts, hose, shirts, and any other accessories. I would not presume to advise women about what to wear except to mention that Brooks Brothers also has a women's department. And remember, there are still people who wear dark suits, black shoes, and white shirts after six. (I once attended a fund-raising dinner that included twenty-seven men from the local monied community; I was the only one in a tan suit, an Oxford cloth blue shirt, and brown shoes. It was a long evening.)

One of the best ways to insure a cold reaction from most of the members of the local hierarchy is to look like you don't know better. Appearance can mean that important invitations are not extended. With people who don't care, what you wear won't matter; with people who do, it can often make an important difference. Why risk compromising a good case when there is something so easy to change about yourself as a narrow rep tie with a four-in-hand knot.

Finally, because of an academic background, many presidents are so facile and clever with words that they deceive both themselves and others on campus about the importance of external affairs. They consider it beneath them or beyond them, and some even think it is relatively unimportant and even trivial. Don't think this way! The position is the result of a mix of fear and a lack of sophistication that can be overcome with an adventuresome attitude and a top advancement staff.

* If people aren't fair, honest, decent, and good, say so.

* The president's main job is off campus; don't be afraid to mingle with strangers.

* Academic freedom is precious; guard it!

* The university is a sanctuary for the presentation of any idea. Don't be afraid to say so.

* Unless in a small town, don't join service clubs, but speak to them.

* Dress, at least a little, like the local aristocracy.

* Spend the entertainment money to boost your stock, not your ego.

* Speak to everyone!

CHAPTER 10

The President and Politicians, Public Figures, and Bureaucrats

Power is the great aphrodisiac.
Henry A. Kissinger

We can't do without dominating others or being served. . . . Even the man on the bottom rung still has his wife or his child; if he's a bachelor, his dog. The essential thing, in sum, is being able to get angry without the other person being able to answer back.
Albert Camus

All men are motivated by self interest: man should play his friends as pawns on a chessboard, one against the other.
Machiavelli

Our sense of power is more vivid when we break a man's spirit than when we win his heart.
Eric Hoffer

POLITICIANS AND PUBLIC FIGURES are probably the easiest to cultivate of any of the hierarchy of the wealthy and powerful. Their positions are modeled from fickle popular opinion. The college or university president also has access to this public and politicians know it—their public is your public. Few

135

members of a general assembly are influenced by the importance of a case to an institution or its president. The case must
be presented in terms of its importance to the public, those
people on whom the public figure depends. Do this and you
will invariably win in the political arena. And the key to doing
this is to win the support and confidence of the general
public—the charismatic president.

Becoming Politically Powerful

Few would debate that power plays a key role in decision making in any arena (Pfeffer, 1981). Speeches in public figures'
districts made to all kinds of groups, including political clubs
and grass-roots organizations such as the American Legion or
Marine Corps League, or religious organizations, will place a
president in contact with the people who form the backbone of
most political organizations.

Political fund raisers on both sides of the aisle are important to attend, and complimentary tickets are easy to get. The
candidate will be pleased to see the college president there
and probably will not realize that he or she is also building a
base of support. This advice is especially important for the
presidents of community colleges and four-year public institutions. During my time in office, in a state with twenty-six
public institutions, I saw only two other college presidents
with any consistency at such functions and they were both
very successful in the state legislature. And the others wondered why.

Take along a small entourage to mix with people and learn
names, interests, and positions. If possible, a public introduction should be arranged subtly through the politician's aid by
an assistant or friend in the group.

In influencing politicians and public figures, newspaper
columns or articles and television and radio appearances can
be especially helpful. A president with a three-minute radio
commentary on the most listened-to local station will find that

no one, including local politicians and newspaper publishers, has more public influence. (More on this later.) At least no one will be *perceived* as having more public influence. People will always be in when that president calls.

Campaign Contributions

Contributing to political campaigns is not a good idea, but if you do, use your own funds and contribute to both candidates. Early in my administration, I got into difficulty by allowing myself to be pressured into buying tickets to an expensive political fund raiser. I rationalized that it was justifiable, for the moment at least, to draw funds from the university foundation to pay for the tickets. The ensuing newspaper publicity dramatized my mistake.

Political Egos

Politicians probably have the largest egos of any influential group, with the possible exception of talk-show hosts. Most are inordinately sensitive and react quickly to slights from anyone outside their hierarchy. Some are abusive, condescending, and rude, but only until you become "somebody" to their constituents.

And do not believe that a college or university president is automatically important to all politicians, public figures, and bureaucrats. To most of them, a president counts for little until he or she actually enters the greater public domain and is known and perceived as being admired. Then, attitudes will suddenly appear to change and the institution's budget proposals pass more easily through legislative committees, as will any other reasonable legislation you favor.

On a personal note, I shall never forget my first appearance before the Joint House-Senate Committee on Budget in the Maryland General Assembly. I had been in office only a few months and was told that I had only twenty minutes to represent the condition, aspirations, and interests of the state's second largest institution to the state's elected representatives. I wrote out every word and rehearsed carefully in front of my bathroom mirror. The presentation was a perfect eighteen minutes, and I thought it was grand. After respectful amenities, I began my splendid address, glancing only occasionally at my prepared text, for I had it memorized by that time. I soon noticed that some committee members were reading newspapers. A little later, the chairman seemed to be engaged in some kind of amorous activity with an attractive administrative assistant. As I launched, disconcerted, into my crescendo, I noted that one committee member was actually asleep. Shaken, I finished to the sonorous tones of the now disengaged chairman who said, "Thank you, doctor, for those eloquent words." On the way back to the campus, I told my associates that they would never again treat our institution or me that way. They didn't.

Politicians and Public Figures on Campus

It is also good to invite public figures to the campus for events that will have large audiences. They often enjoy the activity and always appreciate being introduced. People on campus will be impressed that their president can attract such noteworthy public figures.

On such occasions, a photographer from the institution should always be present to photograph and photograph and photograph. Virtually all of the shots should include the president: in the locker room with the senator and the basketball team, at the reception before the show, playing tennis, or shaking hands at the Christmas party. There should be pictures taken of the president and members of the faculty, student body, and staff. (Always smile, and never be photographed with a glass or cigarette in your hand.) Afterwards, depending on the degree of community sophistication, brief reminders of the occasion can be penned by the president on photos and sent out. Some presidents even frame the photographs before sending them. In time, a president will probably see his or her face hanging on walls in studies, offices, libraries, and dens. When others do the same thing to you, however, don't hang the photograph. It simply tells people who visit your office the people you know who are more important than you. Give autographs, don't ask for them.

The president's office should include tasteful and, if possible, valuable paintings and other art objects, very few school symbols, and not much personal memorabilia. The tone to set is subtle, even diffident and understated.

Compromising Principle

Politicians often have compromised principle somewhere along the road to obtaining or staying in office. Most are nice, outgoing people who have regularly compromised only on issues and positions, but in time most will compromise principles. When politicians get to know a president, many will not hesitate to ask for everything from residence-hall rooms to jobs and special admissions or selection for the sons and daughters of their constituents. Don't do it. Regardless of how important a vote seems, it is never worth it. The president who has successfully gained a reasonable base of popular support won't even be tempted. The president who compromises institutional policies is well on the road to exit from office. Most governors will also test presidents. Treat them no differently than you would a state legislator from a far away district: resist gracefully and try to provide some noncompromising favor instead. Remember that these people stay in their positions largely because of the patronage they can give, and a president who is gullible enough to allow them to use an institution will see it happen. The trust and confidence of associates and people on campus is infinitely more important to a presidency than a favor for the governor or any other powerful figure, but you can gain both and maintain your integrity in the process if you understand and use charismatic power.

Bureaucrats

Bureaucrats are a different breed. Although they often are in company with politicians, they have little in common other than an interest in power. Bureaucrats are often the ones with a state flag on a tie clasp and a rather quiet manner. Although they rarely walk with an air of confidence or authority, many government bureaucrats have the power to break the president of a public institution and they can be painful to presidents in private institutions. They are often unctuous, officious, humorless, and intelligent. Generally, they will convey little respect for a college president or his or her associates. Although there are exceptions, most of them only appear after you become "somebody."

Although the same is essentially true for federal bureaucrats and congressional aides in Washington, D.C., they are sufficiently different to warrant further comment. (Those from the insitution's home town or even state are a different matter, of course.) Because of the size and complexity of the government, their ability, and their staying power, congressional aides in Washington often develop influence beyond that of even some elected officials and should be accorded respect consistent with their achievement. They are usually exceedingly well informed, sophisticated, and occasionally sympathetic. Although a few are interested in a professorship, they are usually impervious to a college president's power and must be approached from a base of expertise. Always know what you are talking about when making a presentation to an experienced congressional staffer. His or her job is based on tenure and expertise, which you can increase by making the staffer look good. Do not be obsequious, for although some congressional staff will act as if they expect you to, you will not be taken seriously if you are. Comport yourself with confidence, charismatic distance, and surety, but be especially certain that the surety is impeccably accurate and substantial.

Catering to Bureaucrats

Presidents and business officers in public institutions and some private are often advised to cater to bureaucrats and to invite them to campus golf courses, football games, private parties, and the like. A few come but the smart ones don't. They want to remain free of obligation, personal or otherwise. Often bright, sometimes informed, and usually completely honest, they feel no anxiety from that quarter. Government policies usually make them immune to dismissal. It is generally a waste of time to curry favor with bureaucrats, who will not respond to charm, flattery, or even respect but will develop, at best, a grudging affection. Presidents so foolish as to grant them favors discover that the bureaucrats do not expect to reciprocate and only feel more contemptuous of their benefactor, and deservedly so.

How to Beat the Bureaucrat

But the higher-ups and top department heads ordinarily are appointed by elected officials, and therein lies the key. If not caught up in the labyrinth of a multilayered state system, the president can beat the bureaucrat by cultivating the people behind the elected officials, thereby winning the top elected officials, the top appointed officials, and, ergo, the bureaucrat. These are easily identified by reading the newspapers and asking people who have been around a while. And they are most effectively impressed by how a college president has cultivated the general community and the media, and may even begin to court him or her as a political candidate. These powerful figures are easier to deal with than their politicians, because they are more secure and therefore less guarded and more candid. Politicians come and go, but power figures usually stay on from administration to administration.

Cultivating the Power Behind the Thrones

Meet them respectfully, but on your own terms. In no way imply a willingness to participate in their "spoils game." They respect a president who isn't brazen about it, and will often grant their favor because he or she might become brazen. They will believe even the president who won't compromise is educable particularly if they see latent political potential. And if you are charismatic, they will see latent political potential even if it's the farthest thing from your mind. And they enjoy being around college presidents just for the company. The word will get around and both the politicians and the bureaucrats will find out. Almost as a bolt from the blue, a public institution's budget documents will no longer be chicken-tracked with red pencil marks, requisitions and requests for new positions will be approved, impressive buildings will be budgeted and built, and budget hearings will run smoothly. And private institutions will find fewer questions raised about public aid to private colleges, cost comparisons, and special capital construction grants. It will not be because the cause has become more worthy, but because the institution's president is now viewed as "somebody."

In summary, politicians, public figures, and bureaucrats are important to the presidents of both public and private institutions, but especially to the presidents of public institutions. They needn't be catered to or feared, but they should certainly be respected and deliberately considered by the president. Because of the great public vulnerability of the politician and the public figure and the dependence of the bureaucrat on both, they as a group can be fairly easily brought into your camp. The key is for you to win the admiration of the persons on whom they depend. Do not waste much time on the politician or public figure alone, for your worthy cause will simply not measure up against their need for public acclaim.

Become charismatic. Be with their people, for they are your people too. The next chapter will suggest in more specific ways the development and shaping up of your presidential image.

* If politics is dirty, you will always need a bath.

* Cultivate the people off campus and the people who control the people whom the people think represent them.

* Never deny convictions for the sake of peace and equanimity.

* Fight issues, not people; never personalize combat.

* Beware of the bureaucrat in a drab suit and a government-seal tie clasp. He's conscientious, usually intelligent, without humor, and generally insensitive to academic matters.

* When undesirable emotion can't be thought away, get deeply involved in unrelated activity.

* Don't get overly serious at social functions.

* With external adversaries, the possibility of war is always better than war itself.

CHAPTER 11

The President and the Media

The greater the power, the more dangerous the abuse.
Edmund Burke, 1771

Omnipotence is bought with ceaseless fear.
Cinna Corneille, 1639

THE PRESIDENT'S OFF-CAMPUS IMAGE is composed of a jumble of impressions formed by a relatively inattentive public. However, this image is the major factor in developing an aura of charisma. In the great majority of cases, print and broadcast media (and especially television) are the prime instruments for creating an image. These forums are to be played as a virtuoso plays a violin, although, like most virtuosos, presidents are seldom satisfied with the reviews. It is not suggested that a direct connection will exist between your public image at any moment and the immediate response you may wish to receive. But the prevailing impression of what a president's standing is with the general public will set the tone and determine the limits of what faculty, students, staff, alumni, trustees, politicians, public figures, bureaucrats, and potential benefactors will do for the president. For even the most experienced, important, sophisticated people make judgments based on how many people admire an individual.

145

The President Can Represent Almost All of the People

It is important to bear in mind that although a president should be alert to his or her standing with the faculty, students, staff, trustees, politicians, and other public figures, they are often a distorting mirror of the president's image or prestige among the public at large. Each has limited and different constituencies and priorities and will typically claim to speak for "their" people, and, quite naturally, purport to be more effective and committed representatives of the people than the president is. They are not. Not if you are doing your job. A president must never even imply this to be the case, even if at any given moment it is, for to do so would obliterate your charismatic potential with whichever group these individuals purport to represent. From that point on, you will be dependent upon the whim of the representative himself for he will clearly know that with his people, he is your master. Remember, they are your people too, or at least potentially they are.

Developing a Presidential Image

Unless leader of a Northwestern or a Johns Hopkins, a president's first moves may not send out ripples that extend far, but, barely discernible as they may be, they are vitally important to the presidency. The public image takes shape the day that an incumbent is first perceived by anyone as the president. This is different from being seen as a scholar, dean, vice president, or public figure in another arena. Once an image of a president is formed, it changes very slowly, if at all. The president who starts off low-key, waiting a while to study conditions before determining a course of action, is almost irreversibly stamped as indecisive and anxious. And for most, this will be true regardless of what is done later.

The public at large whom a president is trying to impress will almost always be preoccupied. Their attention is attracted by what, in journalistic parlance, are called "grabbers"; "my" country, kids, future, present, pocketbook, or pleasures. Anyone who can present these concerns already on their minds as "ours" gains their attention and from there can proceed to convey his or her own particular mission.

A president makes more of an impression by doing than by telling. If a president speaks of challenging antiquated and unproductive conditions, he or she must challenge them. If you're not prepared to do something, don't raise the subject. A president who asks people to give time and effort and doesn't give of himself or herself to the extent possible, shouldn't expect significant contributions. A president should try to find a way to express his or her purpose through personal action that has special meaning to the public, and do so early in the administration. This aspect of leadership is a formidable assignment, for it is competing with daily pressures in the lives of the public as well as with a president's earlier, sometimes too visible performances.

Managing Public Issues

Although a president can control few of the events that command the attention of the people, some issues can be managed. This means depending on happenings beyond your direct control in order to develop either an event or an issue that can be turned to your advantage. Once this step is taken, it can be used as a stepping stone to an ever-widening audience by calling attention either to that issue or to another that is also legitimate and timely. Issues in higher education that immediately suggest themselves are: government ineptitude, bureaucratic inefficiency, political corruption, excessively democratized curricula, uneducated students, declining job markets, student unrest, and reduced government support. The secret here is to get people where they are, and proceed to take them where you will, assuming that the cause is legitimate and worthy. (Sadly, these techniques work whether it is or not.)

Using the Media

The media, the prime instrument for cultivating the greater public, will at times appear as a bane and blessing simultaneously. Presidents are misquoted, misrepresented, distorted, exaggerated, and sensationalized—if they're lucky. When the institution is in trouble, it is the president who is responsible and who has to explain. For better or worse, in the last analysis, the institution's voice is the president's. The president will have an image regardless, so every effort should be made to insure that the image is accurate and enhances the institution's mission and the president's vision.

The Public-Affairs Officer

Here are some guidelines for effective media relations. First, hire a good public-affairs professional. To the astute president, this person is as important as the chief academic officer. In an emergency, the public-affairs officer (sometimes called public-relations officer or public-information officer) is the president's single most important conduit to the public on and off campus. The importance of the president's being free to concentrate on the issues at hand can be offered as the reason for designating a spokesperson.

From the first day, this person should be the institution's official voice. This in no way distracts from the president's identification in the public eye with the institution. A good public-affairs officer is so finely tuned to the presidential role and personality as to quickly develop an almost intuitive sense about the president's best interests—when to speak and when not to. This person is more objective than the president, a presidential assistant, or spouse. The public-affairs officer is the only one fully informed regarding the president and the institution who is able to take the pulse of the media accurately and sensitively. He or she writes well and quickly, performs in crises almost happily, and is completely and totally the president's; if not, hire another one. The public-affairs officer does not pretend to be neutral and, whether or not he or she reports directly to the president's office, has a tested loyalty beyond question. In addition, the good public-affairs professional can assume responsibility for all of the institution's publications and periodicals, direct the president's formal and informal "friend-making" activities, keep an eye on the campus news-paper, and serve as a scapegoat and solver of other com-munication problems that are bound to present themselves.

Like the president's assistant, the public-affairs officer should be encouraged to be ruthlessly frank and candid and to say "you are wrong." Honesty is not disloyalty. There are al-ways people waiting for a president to lose composure or get angry. Under ordinary circumstances, anger might be justifia-ble, but a president only displays emotion publicly after careful thought. The student press can be quite provoking, but the normal tendency to lash out should be controlled. The public-affairs officer will caution a president and help stay the natural need to justify and defend oneself.

Speaking During Periods of Crisis

The question of when to speak is always answered primarily by feeling and intuition. In the last analysis, the president has to make the judgment. The advice and intuition of the public-affairs officer, however, should be heeded above all others.

During periods of difficulty, neither impetuosity nor reluc-tance should determine when to speak. During campus crises or unrest, the president should speak at the peak of the drama, but always let the staff know what he or she plans to say, for they have to handle most of the reverberations. Soldiers should see only stirring and inspiring flashes of the general during combat; to be there all of the time invites the loss of their attention and perhaps their support.

Another good practice is to touch base with leaders on and off campus before announcing major decisions or changes in direction. A president should not appear to be asking what to do too much, but rather, should be more informative than questioning. Tell them why. If this is done effectively, most will be supporters or at least remain silent if defeat or a strong negative backlash results from a presidential action.

Media Appearances

To the extent possible, public media appearances are best staged. Perform on your terms, not theirs. Press conferences are good if media representatives will attend. Calls to sympathetic reporters to offer a story break (about all a president can give a good reporter) will often lead to a favorable story. Regardless of what is written later, people remember the first story. For this reason, a call from the president to previously neutral or even unsympathetic reporters is both surprising and more effective than waiting for them to call. Finally, virtually all invitations to appear on television, radio, or in print should be accepted unless the situation is obviously and completely biased. Try to go on radio and television live rather than taped unless you are assured of a sympathetic reporter.

Reporters

A reporter's job is to report a good story and not to promote an institution or its president. The final test with experienced members of the media is expertise and truth: expert power. Except for the most callow and inexperienced reporter, charisma will buy little with them. Indeed, of all a president's constituent groups, reporters and writers are probably the least impressed by any of the standard measures of power. Legitimate power means little to them unless a president is on intimate terms with their publisher, senior editor, station owner or manager. Even then, a good reporter won't be affected.

Most reporters are inured to rewards. The most professional ones from major news outlets will not accept them; others often take everything from free meals to special passes and even trips, and simply accept the treatment as a matter of course. The rule of thumb is, "The more you give, the less you get." Good reporters think less of those who ply them with rewards, and this lack of respect will somehow creep into what they write. Let relationships with reporters and media personalities be polite but never obsequious and let them develop naturally.

Unfair Treatment by the Media

In case of unfair treatment or misquoting, offending reporters will usually be curt, editors only slightly more polite, and publishers equivocal. It is preferable to talk to those people before rather than after a storm. Although libel charges may seem tempting, try to let the feeling pass as quickly as possible. Newspapers and stations have insurance, and as a semipublic figure, a college president probably won't win anyway. One approach is to meet with members of the editorial staffs to discuss concerns, take them to lunch or dinner, or invite them to social functions—but here again, the good ones usually won't come. Whatever, with representatives of the media be scrupulously honest, be as candid and complete as you can, and don't expect favored treatment. And remember, regardless of what they say, you don't have to talk with them.

The only way to insure fair treatment and perhaps even inspire positive media coverage is to become one of the media yourself and command their attention as a competing power force. To complain about offenses committed by the media gains nothing except a suspicious reputation. On the other hand, the president who has a platform from which to address regularly the same public to which the media appeal implies the threat of retaliation. It is only natural that some reporters have developed arrogant and condescending attitudes for they know that there are few effective checks on their style or substance. But a president who emerges as a well-known, admired, and fair-minded public figure, whether as a commentator on an important radio or television station, a newspaper columnist, or a public speaker, will gain power in any dealings with the media. Editors will speak to you with respect as a peer, reporters will no longer interrupt you in mid-sentence, and publishers will come to hear your speeches.

Other Ways to Insure Objective Media Treatment

Some presidents cannot do these things, sometimes because they have no opportunity but more often because they lack confidence or expertise. There are, however, other reasonably effective ways to accomplish fair and impressive media coverage. It is a given that to do so, a president must be honorable and correct, and an institution engaged in impressive and noteworthy activities. The first and most fragile way to improve an institution's standing with the media is to attempt systematically to cultivate the publisher and the people who influence the publisher, including major advertisers and the local landed gentry, if the publisher is one of them. A president can work to have established some kind of regional or state council to which a person could petition if badly treated by the media. Minnesota has one that has operated effectively for many years. Such a council would consist of prominent people generally beyond the power of the media (for example, major advertisers, retired persons, and religious leaders). Some states, like Florida, have passed redress laws to protect vulnerable public figures, but for the most part the public and particularly those who seek power remain at the mercy of the media unless they enter the arena and gain power for themselves.

This is not to say that a president must become a media personality; rather, an effective presidency is more likely if he or she does. But if the president doesn't, media relations can still be successful; the process will simply require more care and the allocation of even more resources to the public-affairs or institutional-relations office. Good news releases will be even more important, as will special campus features prepared by the public-affairs staff. (A special feature on the president, however, will only get published in the alumni magazine.) A number of universities and colleges have established impressive ways of regularly and quickly conveying newsworthy items to a broad range of print and broadcast media. They use audiocassettes, videotapes, feature idea sheets, opposite editorial page columns, and many other techniques, in addition to standard news releases. (CASE has available specific information and advice regarding techniques to consider in communicating effectively with a diverse public.) Some college and university publications and periodicals are so well done that their readership extends beyond alumni and friends. Many institutions are hiring, as public-affairs officers, people who are not only educated in journalism and experienced in higher education but who have held responsible positions in the media.

As Your Image Develops

As a presidential image begins to develop through the media, do not expect to shape it yourself completely, for no one can fully control what people write or say. Presidents have been called "opportunistic" when they thought they were courageous. A reporter may interpret as "outspoken" a comment the speaker thought was simply truthful. A president may be considered outgoing and assertive who is basically shy and private. The image that comes out may surprise or offend or amuse you. What matters is that you face yourself each morning in the mirror and respect what you see, knowing that you are improving the condition of the institution and the people you serve.

* Don't fall in love with the image of yourself in the first publicity. That way, you can more easily handle what comes later.

* Remember, you don't have to talk to the media, but it's usually a good idea.

* Don't get carried away with your own rhetoric.

⋆ For the president, a feature article in a newspaper is infinitely better than a scholarly piece in a professional journal.

⋆ Don't take it too seriously.

⋆ When they stop calling you outspoken, you've stopped speaking.

⋆ Never apologize for your convictions. If you can't explain them without getting defensive, reexamine them.

CHAPTER 12

The President and Trustees

Yes, power corrupts, but absolute power is absolutely delightful.
Anonymous (Book of Wisdom)

TRUSTEES REPRESENT the most important formal link to a president's supporting public. Most trustees serve because of a special commitment to the institution or the incumbent president, or both, and deserve the definition of the name trustee, which is "to hold in trust." Some serve for reasons of prestige, patronage, power, and personal advantage. Be especially careful of this latter group. Your prime influence with trustees will be charismatic, for to be perceived as such will be to grant your expertise full reign.

Trustees in Public Colleges and Universities

First, a disclaimer about many trustees on the governing boards of public colleges and universities: public trustees are usually elected by the people of the state or appointed by governors or other elected officials as a reward for special service. To suggest that the prime criterion for appointment as a public trustee is the quality and commitment of the candidate is as naive as to suggest that all trustee appointments to the boards of private institutions are made without regard to the personal wealth or influence of the candidate. For these reasons, public trustees are sometimes less committed to their trust and less

155

influential than the trustees of private institutions. Public trustees often have little interest in the institution, and their votes are sometimes significantly influenced by political, business, and personal factors.

This situation is especially prevalent on multischool public boards, the members of which often tend to lack interest and qualifications. For a president to expect helpful support and influence with such a board is almost always detrimental to the institution as well as to the president, for one's charismatic potential is slowly reduced to the level of the persons who serve on the board. Yet these boards do represent the final authority and the president is obliged to show the board its due respect, effectively represent his or her institution in what usually becomes a mediocre concept of public institutions (everything is reduced to a midpoint), and cultivate sufficient external support for the institution to become exceptional—a rather sensitive balance.

These boards often have neither able staff nor trustees sufficiently influential or interested to help the institution. Usually, key decision makers—politicians, state bureaucrats, the media—are also aware that these boards amount to little in the power hierarchy of the state or region. For the president to be obsequious with such boards is to seem inept and impotent by association and eventually to lose the respect of faculty, students, and your associates, as well as off-campus decision makers. And so, be careful: respect your trustees, but remember they are charged to govern several institutions, you are charged to lead one. At times, these can appear to be mutually exclusive functions. Whatever the case, maintain the respect and support of your campus community and the general public, and the sometimes countermoves of the multischool board will not extend too far into your territory.

Not all public trustees are poorly motivated, ill qualified, or unwilling to devote the time and risk necessary to serve a public institution. In many states, however, the committed trustees often end their terms in frustration and cynicism or with a strongly worded letter of resignation. Others just quietly slip away in disgust.

Presidential Power and Trustees

In dealing with trustees, in both private and public institutions, the president must rely almost exclusively on charisma and expertise, but especially charisma. Charisma is generated and made obvious to trustees by strong campus support, and by the admiration of the local, regional, or national hierarchy of the wealthy and powerful. Other external constituent groups—politicians, public figures, alumni, the media, and even bureaucrats—also contribute to the power a president has with a governing board. If trustees perceive the president as effective on campus and respected and influential beyond the campus grounds, assuming that the president is not arrogant or overtly disrespectful, they will give their respect and support, and grant considerable executive privilege.

Board members are admiring and respectful when others perceive their president as a caring individual, a good manager, an inspiring leader, and an influential person off campus. Trustees learn these things from others, not from the president, whose energies will be better spent building a base of support. The president who does these things well doesn't have to worry much about the board. He or she is able to join them as a peer and a leader, and to inspire them to serve a high cause; if not, you are at least able to silence those who would work contrary to your interests.

The President and Trustees

The ideal role and function of the trustee are essentially the same in public and private institutions. Exceptions are primarily in the public sector, where elected and other political figures influence the decisions of trustees. Although the private sector has instances of undue attempts by church members, generous givers, and alumni to influence trustees, these pale when compared to episodes in the public sector. Fortunately, incursions are usually to gain personal and financial advantage rather than to influence academic matters.

Beware of trustees who spend too much time exercising office, especially those who visit the campus frequently and meet in private with administrative officers and faculty. They can do much to reduce virtually all forms of presidential power (legitimate, reward, coercive, expert, and charismatic). And nothing can compromise a president's charismatic power on campus so readily. No one, including few trustees, is as deeply invested in the institution as its president. Faculty members have their disciplines, and trustees are usually at best part-time laypersons committed to the best interest of the institution. The president is at the pinnacle of a career and must be the person in whom the trustees place their authority and much of their power, always excepting, of course, the power to replace the president.

I once worked as a consultant to a community-college president who was having serious leadership problems. The chairman of the board had an office on campus where he spent several hours a week. He visited and discussed college affairs with top administrators, faculty, staff, and students. Of course he was viewed as beyond presidential authority and, in time, his activities significantly undermined the president. The president got into trouble with the faculty and staff of the college and was asked to resign during his third year in office. Four years later, the college was on its third president, and the chairman of the board still had his office on campus.

Other examples of trustees' overinvolvement:

Case 1. *At a midwestern liberal arts college, a wealthy woman who is expected to make a major gift to the college lives in the community and attends most student functions and all student council meetings. At each meeting of the board, she presents a lengthy and even charming report on student behavior at the college and students' relationships with the dean of students and the president. The president and the dean of students sit in board meetings and cringe.*

Case 2. *At a private women's college, the trustee chairing the development committee didn't like the vice president for development, so she worked directly with the several officers who reported to the vice president. She saw the president and all but ignored the* vice president. The president did nothing to reinforce the vice president, who was fired for being ineffective. The vice president's successor seems to be having the same problem and is already in trouble with the president.

Case 3. At a southern Catholic college, several trustees constitute a committee that regularly comes to the campus, has its presence announced, and encourages members of the student body, faculty, and staff to come in and discuss their problems. The trustee committee then reports to the board, and the board doesn't understand why the president can't "lead."

Case 4. The chairman of the board of a Middle Atlantic public university has the habit of inviting groups of faculty to his home for cocktails, dinner, and stimulating conversations. The president of the university not only is not invited, but he must listen to the chairman frequently comment about what the faculty think during public board meetings. The chairman has started discussing the president's limitations with other board members.

These cases are not intended to denigrate the role of the trustee, nor to imply that most are not committed and able. It is a mistake, however, to consider trustees an omnipotent, all-powerful body that must be pleased and adhered to regardless of other considerations. The notion is, quite simply, foolish.

The president's role with trustees should be both professional and personal, but this does not mean sharing everything, either personal or institutional. At the same time, a president should keep no secrets from trustees; rather, tell them more than they want to hear about significant issues, but refrain from discussing personalities at length and administrative procedures, lest you get an overinvolved board and an institution with uncertain direction.

The good president has one-to-one sessions with each of the trustees, and unless the board is unusually large, does so more than once or twice. Playing golf or tennis, attending cultural events and social functions, inviting them to campus social functions (particularly those with the president in the limelight), and performing small noncompromising favors are all worthwhile.

No trustee should be allowed to pressure a president into violating college or university policy, even for something as apparently inconsequential as a room on campus or the admission of a marginal student. Once headed down that road, a president cannot go back, and the trustee served by the compromise will not expect to reciprocate, but will simply assume that favored treatment comes with the trusteeship.

Respectful strength is the most effective presidential posture with trustees. Trustees should be cultivated as well as informed but obsequious deference will not enhance a president's effectiveness. One thinks of the president who laughs too loudly, is too quick to rise, or is overtly attentive. If you catch yourself being that way, stop; it doesn't win anything. Here again, remember that your success and survival depend on the extent to which you are able and willing to define yourself in terms of the interests of people on campus and to maintain the distance necessary to lead. I feel bound to add here that I write this from my position as a trustee of five liberal arts colleges.

The Presidential Power Base

The college president who knows and uses the concepts of leadership and power presented in this book will soon have sufficient stature and influence to be able, if necessary, respectfully to disagree with trustees and, if need be, even with the board itself. Trustees make mistakes, as do presidents, and at times those mistakes will not be effectively corrected by other trustees and must be addressed by the president. If not, you may be assured that things will only get worse. Some presidents have achieved a position of power beyond the collective power of their trustees. In one state, the president of a public institution wanted a separate board of trustees rather than to continue to report to the board that ineptly and corruptly governed seven different universities. His politically appointed board did not agree, yet the strong president was able to generate sufficient support to get a bill passed through the legislature and signed by the governor that created a separate governing board for the university. In this instance, the president had become so influential that he was able to name most of the trustees who were appointed to the board. And throughout the apparent conflict, the president's image and influence appeared so strong that the original board chose not to make a public issue of the matter. The newspapers wrote about it, but the board did nothing. There are countless examples of private institutions where the presidents appear first among equals, and in each instance, the condition has not been achieved by accident.

The fundamental consideration of the president must always be the best interests and welfare of students, faculty, and staff; these clearly stand above the sometimes selfish interests of some members of governing boards. While these kinds of issues should be handled sensitively and the president certainly should not be pushed into a display of bravado, neither should a president pretend that they will go away or that they don't exist. And the extent to which you will be able to be effective in such conflicts will depend almost exclusively upon your ability to foster trust and confidence among the people—charismatic power.

You must establish a broad personal power base that is recognized and subtly acknowledged by the trustees and this will be the degree to which you are able comfortably to maintain your obligation to your faculty, students, and staff. The president must feel able to speak candidly and confidentially to all of the people, and that ability is only insured through achieving a high degree of charismatic power.

Too many presidents sell out their campus people to people off campus. Not only is this ethically questionable, but it will produce a short-term president. This chameleonlike president is either soon detected or, at the luckiest, has a mediocre presidential tenure fraught with anxiety and problems. This is also the president who later writes, too often for publication, that he or she did not enjoy the office. However, the temptation to compromise convictions in the presence of an influential trustee or another off-campus power figure is great. But those who do will find the off-campus power broker's respect short-lived and, in time, will lose the respect and support of other constituencies.

With all these things said about the trustees, you must always know that in the final analysis, the trustees have the authority—the authority to do virtually anything. What the effective president must do is demonstrate by his or her behavior the extraordinary ability that inspires the confidence and respect of the board, and confidence and respect are not earned either by obsequiousness or by intimidation.

Access to the Board

There are almost as many definitions of the proper role of the trustee as there are college presidents and trustees. Nonetheless, the president who understands effective leadership prefers completely informed trustees who are not involved in any way in the administration of the institution. He or she will so state before accepting a presidential appointment, and will occasionally remind, or have reminded, the board of this condition. (Astute trustees will do this for the president.)

Trustees should not be involved in the administration of the institution. Their proper function is to approve policies, evaluate and support or discharge the president, advise the president, and contribute financially or otherwise to the institution. The board should be sufficiently aware to have a good feeling for the institution and what is happening there, but they must not be so involved that they are moved to do things for which the president is ultimately accountable. Some presidents lean toward the belief that trustees should meet to appoint the president, adjourn, send money, and then reassemble only when the president resigns. This stance is probably a bit strong, but it's a good thought to bear in mind while considering trustee involvement in college or university affairs.

The principal informant of trustees should be the president, not other administrators or faculty. There are exceptions, particularly in the private sector, where many development officers, particularly the vice president, need to spend considerable time with trustees. This is why the appointment of a development officer can be crucial to your good administration. (More on this later.)

The wise president guards this relationship with trustees carefully and grants access to them on a very discriminating basis. This in no way suggests a lack of confidence in your campus associates; rather, too much direct contact with the board reduces the president's legitimate and charismatic power (it reduces the board's legitimate power), and it makes the use of all other power forms by the president more difficult. For the best interests of all concerned, the board simply must not usurp the president's responsibilities or in any way replace the president as the chief operating officer of the institution, nor must it give the impression of doing these things.

Keep the board distant from campus people—administrative staff, faculty, and students. Speak of trustees in general, rarely in particular. Conveying a sense of the board's legitimate authority will prove to a president's advantage during periods of difficulty; the president is the key to the trustees' approval, the expert on trustee relations, and the prime determinant of trustee involvement. It is also perfectly legitimate for a president to use the board as a scapegoat for unpopular decisions. A president takes the heat for enough unpopular decisions, so if the opportunity presents itself to use the board, go ahead. Discerning trustees understand this.

The Appointment and Orientation of Trustees

At both public and private institutions, presidents should play a prime role in the appointment of trustees. While building a good board is generally considered a major responsibility of a private institution's president, in the public sector it is often considered presumptuous. A public president, like any other, should do what he or she ethically can to influence the appointment of trustees. If trustees are elected, a president can speak of the qualifications of a good trustee. Once a trustee is on the board, the president will have to live with the choice for a long time; so regardless of custom or method, it behooves a president to be involved.

The education of trustees is as important as their appointment, and the president's task, regardless of resistance, is to insure that they are oriented and informed, a process that begins the day a trustee says yes. There is excellent material available on this and other dimensions of trustee responsibility from the Association of Governing Boards of Colleges and Universities in Washington, D.C.

Fund Raising

Trustees should be exploited—in the best sense—to the advantage of the institution. The president should so inform new trustees and not be reluctant to remind old ones. Whether an institution is public or private, the chair of the board and the president's behavior should diplomatically convey the conviction that the trustee who does not contribute to the institution is unworthy of the appointment. Although some trustees are obviously able to give more than others, all should contribute money, in addition to time and talent. A president who does not gently but firmly convey this to the board will not be well supported. On this it is imperative for the chair of the board to reinforce the president.

To be successful in fund raising, a president must learn to ask for money and not leave the task entirely to trustees, volunteers, or staff. Few development programs are effective without the commitment, leadership, and participation of a strong president. Newly appointed presidents, regardless of experience in fund raising, should appoint a consultant in this area. Get names of consultants from other presidents who are successful in fund raising or contact the Council for Advancement and Support of Education (CASE).

People generally give because of who asks them. Your good

cause is important and so is the sense of obligation or debt a person feels toward your institution, but there is nothing like being asked by the right person. Many times this will be you, sometimes it will be your development officer, but often it will be a person of status and influence more closely akin to the potential contributor's world. Use trustees and other friends of the institution who have already given (preferably more than the person they are going to ask) in this capacity. They can usually raise more money faster and more directly than the grandest case prepared by you, your staff, and your consultant.

It is with the trustees that a president begins the effort to raise money for an institution, for, in spite of the important fund-raising role of others in the local hierarchy of the wealthy and powerful, the core of all really successful fund raising is the governing board of the institution. If trustees are not accustomed to giving or feel no responsibility, the president's task is to educate them to the fundamental importance of this role and to be certain that they are asked to give. Trustees simply must give to the institution and any who don't should be counted as presidential failures. Trustees should be deeply involved in, but not accountable for, everything from annual funds to capital campaigns to planned giving and even phonathons.

As the essence of the institution, the president inspires donor confidence and creates the climate in which fund raising takes place. Trustees bear a measure of the responsibility, but the president brings it into focus. Fund raising cannot be completely delegated to anyone, not even to an extraordinarily competent vice president.

An axiom of fund raising is that no program achieves success without strong leadership by the board of trustees, or, in the public sector, by the board of an institutionally related foundation. To the extent possible, the president should carefully assemble a board of trustees that will contribute and be involved in fund-raising activities. A background in some kind of successful voluntary fund raising and substantial personal means are important. After their selection, trustees should be carefully educated as to the nature and needs of the institution. There are those who say that selecting trustees who can both get and give is the major responsibility of the president.

More difficult for the president of a public institution, careful trustee selection and orientation is important nonetheless. Public college and university presidents are more frequently using private foundations created exclusively for their institutions for generating private resources. Although the practice is rarely as effective as involving trustees, it may be necessary, particularly for the president with a multischool board. But even so, trustees should not be let off the hook. This also applies to community-college presidents. And one or more of the trustees should be members of the foundation board.

Professional expertise, however, is again important. If a foundation is created without the sufficient involvement of experts, the most uncomfortable but important element, giving, is likely to be left out. People think they don't need to give to a public institution, and many presidents don't know how to ask; they postpone asking, thinking they will raise the subject after they educate their prospect, when in fact all this does is make more remote the prospect's ever giving. Thus, presidents have ended up with a foundation board of influential and wealthy people who either don't give enough or don't give at all. Another potential drawback of foundation boards is that they can become too autonomous. Ordinarily, the chief development officer should also be the board president or executive vice president. If not, the president could end up petitioning another board for support, and the fund-raising program could lose its vitality. The important thing here is that you not lose the reins of your board.

Finally, it is important that the development staff adjust its style and presentations to the president, not vice versa. While candor from the chief development officer should be encouraged, do not be overly influenced by experienced officers who counsel doing it their way. Listen, learn, and then do it the way that is most comfortable. Fund raising is rarely the happiest part of a presidential tenure, but it can be fun; there are few feelings more exhilarating than bringing in the big gift.

The Development Office

As has been suggested, one of the first things a newly appointed president should do is assess the condition of the development office, and this can be done most astutely by appointing an experienced consultant. (Good consultants include both full-time consultants and experienced development officers at other institutions—remember you can call CASE for advice.) Your next step is to be certain that you have a good chief development officer. The best way to assess an institution's development operation is to examine the record. If there isn't one, the situation usually calls for quick changes. Remember that in development it is necessary to spend money to make money. Suppress the reluctance to allocate the funds, defend the allocation to trustees and administrative staff, hold the chief development officer completely accountable, and listen to him or her. I remember too well not heeding the recommendations of my vice president for development who, year after year, urged the appointment and training of a full-time planned-giving officer. If I had, we would have had hundreds of thousands of additional unrestricted dollars. It still hurts. The general rule in fund raising is that a substantial investment in a new or dramatically changed development office takes about three years to begin to pay off; from then on, the institution benefits materially. You should also bear in mind that your institutional friend-raising activities are essential to successful fund raising. These activities are focused in a public-relations office and an alumni office; both should be effectively related to your development operation.

At most institutions, development—or institutional advancement—is a line division reporting to the president in the same fashion as academic affairs, student services, business and operations, or any other top line function. Your vice president of development can represent the difference between your tenure being good or distinguished; and for more and more institutions, it means the difference between success or failure. Your best advice here is to take all of your advancement functions, public relations, alumni, governmental relations, publications, and the like, and assign them to one area headed by a vice president for development (or advancement). This more clearly forces all of these activities to be evaluated in terms of bottom-line fund raising. This is not to suggest that everything should be reduced to how much money it brings in, but it is to say that most presidents do not pay enough attention to translating communication and friend-making activities into dollars and cents for the institution. The best way to solve the problem and eliminate petty conflict is to make one officer accountable for both your friend-raising and fund-raising activities.

The Vice President for Development or Institutional Advancement

A vice president for development is not employed for a pittance. Development is the most immediately measurable of any vice-presidential division; either it raises money or it doesn't. Good vice presidents of development are worth the investment; some presidents even pay development vice presidents, like some football coaches, more than their own salaries and include perks to match their own. One midwestern liberal arts college president, after offering more money and more perks, finally offered a candidate for development vice president his office. The candidate didn't take the job.

Complete confidence in the chief development officer is fundamental. The ideal candidate offers good sense, organizational skills, and fund-raising experience. The candidate should seem likely to wear well with the president's constituency and the president. Look into the situation where the person worked previously. Has he or she truly led an impressive fund-raising campaign, or was the success due to one or two "angels" or some other factors?

If a person with strong experience cannot be found, don't despair. After becoming discouraged in my first search for a vice president for development, I finally appointed a faculty member of an English department who had successful experience in private business management, who was especially interested in the institution, and with whom I felt a warm and special chemistry. He studied, attended professional meetings and conferences, and we appointed a consultant. A few years later, our university (among institutions of its kind) had achieved number-three ranking in nonalumni giving, had received one of the top two national awards in community relations, and had received several national awards for its publications. He is now the vice president for development of an important liberal arts college and enjoying even greater success.

Once a top-flight development vice president is in place, the president and vice president can begin to develop and implement a design for successful fund raising, usually in conjunction with a tested consultant. Although the institution and the president should be the focus of most fund-raising activities, an able development staff must be there, researching, planning, coordinating, cultivating, and often pointing the president in the right direction and literally moving your lips.

The Board Meeting

The executive committee of the board should meet or consult prior to the board meeting and should usually meet, albeit briefly, at the time of the meeting itself. The executive committee should include key and experienced members of the board who have the confidence of both the president and the chairman of the board. Always be certain that the executive committee, especially the chairman of the board, is fully informed about all potential problems. Don't assume that they don't want to know or that you shouldn't tell them. They will come to know you almost as well as your vice presidents and presidential staff, and will be a significant test of your charismatic leadership, for you have virtually no legitimate power with them. But, if you are successful with your other constituencies and you bear in mind the prime charismatic feature of distance, you will have a good and happy relationship with your key trustee leadership.

Board committees should meet at the time of the board meeting. This insures good attendance, continuity, and saves time and money. The committee meetings should precede the board meeting, and the trustee chair of the committee should report at the full board meeting rather than the vice president or other administrator who staffs the committee. Some presidents find it of value to include the committee chairs as members of the executive committee, although this can lead to cumbersome and unwieldy executive committee meetings and some use steering committees that include the committee chairs and the executive committee.

The opening session of the board should begin with an inspiring and brief presidential report on the state of the institution. Your written presidential report to the trustees in advance of the meeting should always include sections on each of the major activities (usually the line divisions) and cover other general subjects affected by board policy. Oral reports on each division should be presented by the trustee chair of each committee, which occasionally the president may amend or call on an appropriate vice president to explain further. Most presidents put the development committee's report too far down the agenda and, as a result, trustees are unable to give full and enthusiastic attention to this fundamental area. Development should follow the academic affairs report and should never be lower than third on the agenda.

Unless pressed or irrevocably hostage to prior unwise commitments, it is usually best not to have faculty or students attend or make reports at board meetings, nor should they be members of board committees. Quite simply, such practices threaten to erode the president's influence (and charismatic potential) with both groups. If anything, have them make reports to board committees. If you are unable to accomplish these conditions, know that all of your power forces with the board will be somewhat compromised, and executive sessions with the board become even more important for you.

Executive Sessions of the Board

At formal trustee meetings, an executive session that excludes the vice presidents and others is important. During these sessions, you can discuss whatever strikes you at the moment as being of sufficient weight. Although occasionally there may be nothing to report, include the item on the board agenda anyway; it keeps the vice presidents and others aware of their president's mystique and exclusive authority. Executive sessions of the board may also be called during emergencies.

Trustee Disagreements and Spokespersons During Trouble

Unless there is absolutely no alternative, a president never gets involved in disagreements among trustees. While playing the role of mediator or even taking sides may be tempting, in the end, it will almost invariably be the president who suffers. If trustee conflicts become so serious that the president's office can't be effectively conducted, call the Association of Governing Boards or your national presidential association for advice about choosing an outside consultant.

Should an institution encounter the kind of trouble that commands media attention, the president or an agent—not board members—should speak to the media. Try to obtain an understanding or even a policy from the board that asks trustees to make "no comment" and refer inquiries to the president's office. If possible, the only times a trustee should speak to the media are at the request of the president and when the president is under fire and needs support. In these unusual circumstances, the trustee should speak at a press conference arranged by the president's press officer. And, except in rare instances, the speaker should be the board chair.

In sum, trustees should be respectfully dealt with as the designated representatives of the supporting and concerned public of the institution, but the approach should be that of one in the company of peers. This can only be accomplished with any degree of surety if the president has built a base of support that includes the campus constituency and the off-campus individuals and groups who are of special importance to the trustees.

* All trustees give. If they don't, it's your fault.

* It is better to miss a board meeting than a funeral.

* When tempted to compromise by governing boards, politicians, or others in power, keep faith with students, faculty, and staff.

* Don't be afraid to admit mistakes, just don't make them often.

* Appoint consultants because you need their support as well as their expertise.

CHAPTER 13

The President and the Alumni

Power is the ability to show up late for a meeting and have the people thrilled when you arrive.

Louis XIV

Keep 'em a little nervous.

Robert Forman

ALUMNI ARE THE CONSTITUENCY a president is most likely to take for granted. Yet, without a strong and positive base of alumni support, a president is bound to fail in virtually any effort to enhance his or her charismatic power. Whether alumni are of modest achievement and means or rich and powerful, they must not be overlooked in favor of other external groups. Without their interest and involvement, a president can neither gain lasting friends among nonalumni, generate a broad base of public support, raise money from nonalumni benefactors, nor significantly influence trustees, politicians, or the media.

Alumni are "grown-up" students, and whatever else they become, remain students until the day they die. Indeed, it often seems as if a cycle were at work. Many undergraduates become intensely committed to their institutions, leave after graduation or for other reasons, apparently with only passing interest in their former schools. As the years go by, however, they return to their alma mater fired with appreciation and interest. It is this spirit that a president should ethically exploit to the fullest.

173

A wise president communicates honestly and completely with alumni, even if the news isn't always popular. That is why the first steps with alumni are so important. It is only logical that most alumni remember their alma mater as it was, and want it to stay as they remember it. The president's plans must be presented as ways to make the alma mater even more excellent while preserving and respecting many of the old traditions. There is a tendency among alumni to resent dramatic changes—even new presidents—that may develop if warm and convivial relationships with the alumni leadership are not immediately established by a new president.

Alumni Associations

Most colleges and universities cultivate their alumni communities through the creation of alumni associations. These are staffed by professional officers charged with representing either the alumni or the institution or both. This is an easy relationship until there is conflict, an inevitable circumstance between alumni and a changing institution. For this reason, the alumni officer at a dynamic institution has perhaps the most schizophrenic position of anyone on the institution staff. Regardless of the nature of the alumni association, for a president to constrain the officer to the same absolute conditions of staff loyalty expected of other staff is to render the alumni officer finally ineffective in working with this key constituency.

Whatever your experience with and attitudes toward alumni associations, do not rush off pell-mell upon appointment and abruptly change its nature. Any changes in this area should come only after strong relationships are firmly established with key alumni leaders. Presidents who encounter difficulties with alumni aren't saved by the support of the governing trustees. To seek their assistance may actually cause greater harm. Alumni do not fear trustees, staff, faculty, big givers, politicians, or a president. It is their hearts that are vested in the institution. Presidents who have offended alumni have literally been driven from office. A president has legitimate, reward, and expert power with alumni only so long as they agree with him or her. Coercive power is virtually nonexistent. A president must rely almost exclusively on his or her ability to develop charismatic power. Initially, trustees grant the new president a certain grudging respect, but their affection and support must be won. Perhaps more than anyone else, alumni must trust and like the president before really giving their support. Without it, a short term lies ahead.

Independent and Dependent Alumni Associations

Most alumni associations depend on the institution for support and staff. Others are partially independent, and a few provide for themselves completely. The prime source of support for the alumni association doesn't matter. What counts is to have alumni involved in a serious and constructive manner in the affairs of the institution.

With independent associations, the risk is run of less efficiency and of an association's developing so much autonomy that it becomes an unrestrained adversary. The staff officers of independent alumni associations do not report to the president but to their alumni boards. However, although this can produce anxious moments, in reality it may prove to the president's advantage. If a president is willing to gamble on his or her charismatic skills, an independent alumni association can become the most effective milieu for cultivating alumni support. Alumni of public institutions will often give more under such a relationship. If the president is perceived as a more confident and open president, the alumni association, the institution, and the president will prosper.

Should the more comfortable, dependent association structure be chosen, the result need not be dramatically less productive. The imperative here is that the president realize that the paid alumni officer must honestly render to the president or a delegate the attitudes and opinions of alumni. While the alumni officer may be expected to represent the interests of the institution to alumni, he or she must also be able to represent the interests of the alumni in a way that is reassuring to them. Although alumni do not mind being influenced or persuaded, they will not accept coercion at all. Information and persuasion must be applied to convince alumni that the president's way is best. The presentation should not invite disagreement, but inform convincingly.

Alumni and especially alumni officers realize that their interests are better served if the incumbent president of the alma mater receives their support. There is no case with which I am familiar in which an alumni association took the first step towards a hostile relationship with a new president. Most alumni associations will let the president do as he or she pleases, so long as it is done with thoughtfulness and care.

Cultivating Alumni

The charisma established on campus and with other external groups will be helpful in developing good relationships with alumni. However, attention is due to the special importance of an institution's alumni, and the president must make the alumni know how important they are. This applies regardless of whether alumni are genuinely accomplished or of modest achievement and means. Of course, the president should be presidential with alumni, and distance, trappings, ceremonies, and other charismatic qualities apply as much to alumni as to other groups.

A variety of approaches to alumni are effective, such as special letters and off-campus speeches to alumni groups— but should not be so frequent or regular as to become taken for granted. Occasionally, a president can attend part of an alumni board meeting to make a brief presentation. One-to-one sessions with important alumni leaders include visits to their homes and offices. Attending virtually all campus alumni functions, campus athletic activities, and other events where large numbers of alumni may be present will help to build support.

The Alumni Officer

If a president inherits a chief alumni officer of senior tenure, he or she should try to keep the person aboard. Experienced alumni officers will respect a new president and are prepared to be supportive. However, perhaps more than anyone else on the staff, alumni officers have a deep and abiding affection for the institution, and a new president wisely makes serious efforts to convey the same feeling to them. They often have closer ties in the alumni community than anyone else on campus or off.

Should the inherited alumni officer be inexperienced, educate him or her as quickly as possible. What comes naturally simply doesn't effectively realize full alumni potential. Send the alumni officer to professional meetings and especially to special conferences designed to instruct alumni officers in appropriate techniques. Encourage them to read professional magazines, articles, and books. (Further information is available on this subject through the Council for Advancement and Support of Education.) Foster the continuing education of alumni staff, and soon, alumni will be contributing as never before.

If a president needs to appoint a new alumni officer, it is essential that alumni play an important role in the selection process, even in dependent associations in which the president makes the final decision. (An independent association should be so structured that the president has a voice in the appointment of a new alumni officer.) The important condition is that a committee on selection be created to which the college president has an appointment. If one person can't represent a president's interests, then either serious mistakes have already been made with alumni or the wrong person is on the committee.

Alumni Publications

The alumni publication may be put out by the alumni office or the publications staff. This is a valuable public-relations tool and should be furnished sufficient resources for excellence. This doesn't require that it be elaborate or expensive, but that the writing and design reflect the quality of the academic program. Have someone talk with the editor about ways the president can be prominently portrayed in the publication. "A Message from the President" in every issue could get boring unless the incumbent is an exceptionally skilled writer. Instead, strive for a variety of coverage: a picture at a newsworthy campus event, an article by the president, and a report on a presidential speech. The president wants to be prominent, but a skillful editor can help insure this spells "leadership" rather than "ego."

If the association is independent, the same kind of coverage is desirable but more subtlety may be required to obtain it. Presidents have no editorial authority over publications, nor should they have. But if a president is becoming a public figure and providing strong leadership, he or she will naturally make news that the independent alumni association periodical will want to cover. An unfettered alumni press inspired by a dynamic president will, in any case, yield better results than a restricted editor putting out what amounts to a tired house organ—such censorship is always obvious.

Alumni are older students over whom a president has no real authority but who, mobilized and committed, can be a crucial force in achieving institutional goals. Alumni are educated and, in most circumstances, rational people, except when it comes to their alma mater. The old school can bring tears, and don't forget it. Respect, include, and understand alumni. In almost every group a president addresses, someone will hear the words in that context. When addressing a group exclusively composed of alumni, a president should not talk only about the university or the college today, but also of history, tradition, and customs, as well as former faculty and even presidents. Show slides and films, but always include monuments and reminders of the past. Do these things, and alumni will love you.

* Your alumni want to love you.

★ Never, never compromise principle, no matter what the temptation.

★ Drink club soda and lime at most social functions. Afterward, take a stiff belt.

★ With alumni, try to discuss travel, children, the weather, and almost anything else, but be careful of athletics and politics.

★ Always wait overnight or longer before posting a nasty letter.

★ Remember, dignity can also be fun.

CHAPTER 14

Review and Reflections

To know the pains of power, we must go to those who have it; to know its pleasures, we must go to those who are seeking it.

No man is wise enough nor good enough to be trusted with unlimited power.

Charles Colton, 1825

Be cheerful while you are alive.
Ptahhotpe, 24th Century B.C.

THE THESIS OF THIS BOOK is contained in the opening analogy of St. Simone who, after twenty years of trials on a platform sixty feet in the air, declared, "The most difficult part was getting on top of the platform." So it is with many college presidents who, because of background, inexperience, and lack of orientation, find themselves ill prepared for their vital leadership roles in colleges and universities. Indeed, they often find that they just aren't up to their jobs. The purpose of this book has been to help you as a president to do an effective job. It was written by a psychologist who reveled in the presidential role for almost a decade and who attempted to apply much of the research on leadership and power to the exercise of that office. The book was written from the certain conviction, tested in practice, that if one is sufficiently bold and compassionate, few will be strong enough or care enough to question seriously the exercise of that leadership and power—unless, of course, you write a book about it. The job was also fun, and is recommended to thoughtful persons without the slightest reservation. If you don't take yourself

181

too seriously in the process, you'll be able to step down from the platform and walk away with a smile that will say it all.

Setting the Stage

The first chapter is designed to catch your attention and interest. Starting with St. Simone, a discussion is joined about how tough the job of president is and how poorly prepared most are when they are appointed. An attempt is made to dramatize presidential mistakes that would not have been made had the presidents in question known and understood the concepts of leadership and power discussed in this book. The case for leadership and especially power is then presented. The chapter closes with a strong statement emphasizing the importance of understanding and using tested concepts of power in an effective presidency.

Chapter 2 continues to build the case for thoughtful attention by citing much of the current writing about the generally lamentable state of presidential leadership in higher education. Further information about the nature of the presidency is cited as are writers who rationalize the ineffective president by saying that our times neither invite nor require strong presidential leadership. Several citations from other generally respected sources speak to the contrary—that strong presidential leadership will be the imperative of the future for higher education. Closing this section with a recent Harvard symposium on leadership, which concluded that we must have "crusader" presidents in the future, the remainder of the chapter is devoted to a discussion of great college and university presidents and to a succinct review of the current research on effective leadership.

Chapter 3 is the *pièce de résistance*. It is intended to be the most exhaustive review of the research on power applied to the college presidency done to date. (It may have succeeded because, to my knowledge, none has ever been attempted before.) This chapter, the objective rationale for my subjective interpretations on virtually all subjects affecting the university and the president, is the bulwark of all that follows. All forms of influence or power are presented under one or more of the five rubrics—coercive, reward, legitimate, expert, and referent or charismatic power. Research in each of the forms of power is discussed with special attention to implications for the college presidency. Each of the forms of power is applicable to the presidency, but the most significant are in this order: charismatic (the ability to inspire trust and confidence), expert, legitimate, reward, and coercive. Because of its basic importance to the college president, charisma is discussed at great length, including its three principal characteristics: distance, style, and perceived self-confidence—but especially distance because of its importance and its uncomfortable connotations. The chapter ends with a list of conclusions drawn from the research on power. Bear in mind, this is the chapter that inspires virtually all of the succeeding chapters.

The Application of Power

In Chapter 4, an effort is begun to translate through experience and informed speculation the research on power and leadership. Little effort is made to document specifically or to cite confirming examples, for, in the larger measure, the suggestions speak from an integration of the research and personal experience, and as such they stand or fall. (And in response to criticism, I shall have the assertion of the surviving veteran, "Well, it worked for me!")

This chapter, "The Charismatic President," includes all of those areas and activities that do not seem to fall under a specific category to be discussed later. These are things that, if handled properly, will inspire and foster a charismatic presidency: presidential behavior; speaking engagements and ceremonies; adversaries; the president's vision; taking yourself too seriously; demagogues, zealots, and martyrs; the value of conflict; overexposure and charisma; labor disputes; and the importance of the people. Through the discussion, you should bear in mind each of the power forms, and particularly the key charismatic qualities of distance, style, and perceived self-confidence.

Power Inside the Institution

The next four chapters (5 through 8) deal with your several internal constituencies: the administration, institutional governance, faculty, and students.

The administration is your team; administrators should either agree with you, change your mind, or resign. The president should make the final decision on all administrative appointments. In such a system, it is essential that superior persons be appointed to administrative positions.

Those faculty and students affected by decisions should have a voice in their making, but the president should have final authority over all campus issues. You and other administrators should not vote in campus-governance mechanisms; this leaves you ethically free to influence the votes of those who do.

Faculty should expect complete academic freedom in the expression and interpretation of their subjects; but in matters of academic administration, there must be sufficient structure and administrative authority to present majority positions, facilitate the play of influence and power, and encourage decision making.

Students should be listened to and understood, but required to submit to the educational experiences finally deemed appropriate by the faculty and approved by the president. Of course, students should be an official part of the primary governance body of the institution, in addition to having their own governance system.

Subjects also considered are: the house-appointed president; presidential associates; the organization of the administration; socializing with staff and the role of the spouse; close friends and intimacy; loyalty; the role of top associates; handling coalitions; the person who denigrates your predecessor; appointing new administrators; when to appoint an executive vice president; the value of a presidential assistant; delegation; a president's council; the nature and role of a chief academic officer; administrative salaries; the use of presidential vetoes; how to influence your assembly; collective bargaining; speaking to the assembly; governance in more complex institutions; relationships with faculty leaders; staying in touch with faculty opinion; faculty parties; the president and student activities, in the residence hall and other campus centers; the president and student leaders; student unrest; and the role and nature of your chief student-services officer.

In each of these chapters, an effort was made to relate the various power forms to the role of the president and especially to demonstrate how to make optimal use of charismatic power. In effect, you are advised, "Do these things well, and you will have the trust and confidence of your people." And you will deserve it. Of course, you have at your disposal all other forms of power, but the key to effectively developing a base of charismatic and expert power is to use legitimate, reward, and coercive power sensitively. For example, almost anyone willing to pay the price of distance can be charismatic, but it's easier to do so from a legitimate structure that allows you the authority to reward and punish. (The degree to which you are charismatic is the degree to which you will be able to negotiate that legitimate structure and therefore be granted the exercise of your vision.) Expert and charismatic power are incremental kinds of influence that are granted to those who become virtuosos in the legitimate arena. But virtually anyone can become a leader and exercise power. All it takes is the knowledge and some practice—but it helps if you are a college president.

Power Outside the Institution

Chapters 9 through 13 discuss power off campus and treat the president's role with: persons of influence, politicians, public figures, bureaucrats, media figures, trustees, and alumni. Although you have some of the other power forms off campus, you must rely on even larger measures of charismatic and expert power, for, in actuality, off campus you have little legitimate or reward power, and almost no coercive power.

The key to influencing all external decision makers will be the extent to which you can appeal to them on their terms. You need to use everything from dress to becoming a media personality. To be effective externally, you as president will literally have to go public. For instance, if a politician believes that the people who elect him or her really support you, you will find your meritorious position much more readily accepted. This means that you should learn to be a more effective public speaker and accept, even seek, all kinds of speaking invitations. Show up at political rallies and speak to political clubs (both parties). Write newspaper features and, in time, even a regular newspaper column, or do your own radio or television show (especially television). Never turn down opportunities for solo media appearances, and always know what you are talking about. Give sermons in the local churches and temples; speak to the Marine Corps League as well as the Junior League, the Junior Chamber of Commerce as well as the Rotary Club; and be introduced at political fund raisers. Be out, be seen, and be heard! Share your vision.

Never try to intimidate the media in the name of fair treatment, or in any other name, for that matter. There are only two ways to beat the media. You can become such an honorable and impeccable public figure that they dare not write distorted or inaccurate things about you (and this image is almost impossible for any real activist, especially early on). Or you can enter the media business yourself and become a force to be reckoned with. Media writers will not be impressed with you, but their publishers and station owners will, because you are now in a position to question the credibility of their work. Credibility amounts to circulation, and circulation and advertising are the bottom line for media owners. But, whatever you do with the media, do not expect the fact that you are a college president to impress them. And don't try the argument that they should write about good news rather than bad. Even when your excellent staff writes interesting features for the media, writers, editors, and radio and television reporters will still be primarily attracted to the problems you and the institution encounter. Other techniques for effective use of the media in this chapter include: the use of press releases, entertaining media representatives, media councils, and public-relations staff.

Although trustees are to be respected and nourished, you should work with them as equals. (You'll know if you're being too obvious.) All trustees must give money to your institution. The trustee who doesn't give should be counted a presidential failure. Learn to ask. And then get your big givers to ask for you, particularly the chair of your board. You ought to appoint a consultant in fund raising soon after taking office because it's here that most presidents fall short, and they often realize it too late. A number of rules for your relationships with trustees are discussed in Chapter 12, all of which are the result of experience, observation, reading, and a sense of the research on effective presidential power. But first among these rules is that trustees must not dabble in the administration, and, with the help of your board chairman, you as a newly appointed president should thoughtfully and quickly put together a design that prevents this likelihood. This also means that trustees should not be officially involved in administrative or faculty appointments or evaluation; indeed, the trustee's prime conduit to the institution should be the president.

And finally, alumni are discussed, who are—and always will be—your grown-up students. They will grant you legitimacy so long as you have their trust and confidence—so long as you are charismatic. You can be viewed as charismatic by alumni by being committed to their alma mater (what it was, as well as what you want it to be), respecting them as important and continuing members of the college or university community, allowing them to be involved in worthwhile activities, and giving them the feeling that they are important to you. You will be important to them if you do these things and remember to keep your distance. Bear in mind that you are still their president, and they will support you if you give them a chance. And always remember that before you can gain the lasting support of any other external constituency, you must have the support of your alumni, regardless of how modest their achievements. Alumni, like students, remain the heart of the institution. Also discussed in this chapter are the role of the alumni officer, dependent and independent alumni associations, and alumni publications.

These chapters dealing with external affairs also discuss: the problems of the intellectual president; the role of institutional advancement; some general principles of external relations; being comfortable as the star of the institution; cultivating your "who's who"; accepting appointments to boards and commissions; joining country clubs and service clubs; bringing power people to the campus; the value of "one on one"; presidential dress; how to become politically powerful; contributing to political campaigns; massaging political egos; compromising principle; the differences between federal and state and local bureaucrats, and how to beat them; how to represent all of the people; developing your presidential image; managing public issues; the important role of your public-affairs officer; when to speak during periods of crisis; the role of reporters; taking your image too seriously; problems with trustees of public institutions and how to handle them; your power base with trustees; granting access to the board; the appointment and orientation of trustees; your chief development officer; who speaks for the board; board meetings; and the value of executive sessions.

Here again, although not often specifically cited, the fundamental and incremental value of charismatic leadership is implicit in virtually everything advised about the role of the president in external affairs. You must have the support, confidence, respect, and, to the extent possible, even the affection of all of your external publics. You will not win them by rolling over and playing dead on call, engaging in fierce, direct combat, or by ignoring them out of anxiety and not knowing what to do. You win public figures by maintaining a strong base of campus support and by a dual process of engaging their public as you engage them. In your role, you will bring into play virtually all of the power forms: all of the charisma and expertise you can muster, as much legitimate power as you can foster and your board will grant, a touch of reward power that is both effective and reasonably safe, and an occasional trace or reminder of your ability to punish or withhold recognition.

Do not assume in your consideration of charisma that you are less because of your ethical staging. There is no such thing as a charismatic leader who hasn't done what you are doing; they all know that familiarity breeds debate, and they are careful about whom they are familiar with. Never forget the basic and prime charismatic characteristics of distance, style, and perceived self-confidence—and especially distance. Remember, as president, you don't have colds, fatigue, or serious problems. When you are tempted to speak of your terrible burdens to one you should inspire, pick up the telephone and call another president.

Whatever course you choose, I hope that reading this book has given you cause to think and perhaps to smile. If it has done that, it has been worth the writing.

- ★ Familiarity breeds too much.

- ★ If you find yourself unburdening your problems too often and too much, it's probably time to leave office.

- ★ Laugh, especially at yourself.

- ★ Keep reading.

- ★ Listen.

- ★ When your stock is down, don't expect too many friends to step forward; count as precious that small handful who do.

- ★ There can be an exception to every rule.

- ★ When I leave office, please let me slip out quietly. If you're going to give me a gold watch, send it.

- ★ Care.

- ★ Smile.

Bibliography

ALINSKY, S. D. *Rules for Radicals.* New York: Random House, 1972.

ALLEN, R. W.; MADISON, D. L.; PORTER, L. W.; RENWICK, P. S.; and MAYER, B. T. "Organizational Politics: Tactics and Characteristics of Its Actors." *California Management Review* 22(1979):77–83.

ARGYRIS, C., and CYERT, R. M., eds. *Leadership in the '80s.* Cambridge: Harvard University Institute for Educational Management, 1980.

ARGYRIS, C., and SCHON, D. A. *Theory in Practice: Increasing Professional Effectiveness.* San Francisco: Jossey-Bass, 1974.

ASTIN, A. W. *American Freshman: National Norms.* Cooperative Institutional Research Program, University of California-Los Angeles, 1981.

ASTIN, A. W., and SCHERREI, R. A. *Maximizing Leadership Effectiveness.* San Francisco: Jossey-Bass, 1980.

BAKER, L. C.; DiMARCO, N.; and SCOTT, W. E. JR. "Effects of Supervisor's Sex and Level of Authoritarianism on Evaluation and Reinforcement of Blind and Sighted Workers." *Journal of Applied Psychology* 60(1975):28–32.

BALDRIDGE, J. V.; CURTIS, D. V.; ECKER, G.; RILEY, G. L. *Policy Making and Effective Leadership.* San Francisco: Jossey-Bass, 1978.

BANKS, W. C. The Effects of Perceived Similarity and Influencer's Personality upon the Use of Rewards and Punishments. Paper read at Eastern Psychological Association Meetings, Philadelphia, Pennsylvania, 1974.

BARR, B. M. *Leadership, Psychology and Organizational Behavior.* New York: Harper, 1960.

BENEZET, L. T.; KATZ, J.; MAGNUSSEN, F. W. *Style & Substance: Leadership and the College Presidency.* Washington, D.C.: American Council on Education, 1981.

BERKOWITZ, L., and DANIELS, L. R. "Responsibility and Dependency." *Journal of Abnormal Sociology* 66(1963):429–36.

BERLE, A. *Power*. New York: Harcourt, Brace, and World, 1967.

BIERSTADT, R. "An Analysis of Social Power." *American Sociological Review* 15(1950):730–38.

BIRD, C. *Social Psychology*. New York: Appleton-Century, 1940.

BLAKE, R. R.; MOUTON, J. S.; and WILLIAMS, M. S. *The Academic Administrator Grid*. San Francisco: Jossey-Bass, 1981.

BLAU, P. M., and SCOTT, W. R. *Formal Organizations*. San Francisco: Chandler, 1962.

BURKE, P. J. "Authority Relations and Disruptive Behavior in the Small Group." *Dissertation Abstracts* 26(1966):4850.

———. "Authority Relations and Disruptive Behavior in Small Discussion Groups." *Sociometry* 29(1966):237–250.

BURKE, W. W. "Leadership Behavior as a Function of the Leader, the Follower, and the Situation." *Journal of Personality and Social Psychology* 33(1965):60–81.

CAPLOW, T. *Two Against One: Coalitions in Triads*. Englewood Cliffs: Prentice-Hall, 1968.

CARBONE, R. F. *Presidential Passages*. Washington, D.C.: American Council on Education, 1981.

———. Personal conversation, 1982.

CARP, F. M.; VITOLA, B. M.; and McLANATHAN, F. L. "Human Relations Knowledge and Social Distance Set in Supervisors." *Journal of Applied Psychology* 47(1963):78–80.

CHICKERING, A. W. *The Modern American College*. San Francisco: Jossey-Bass, 1981.

CLARK, B. R. "Organizational Adaptation and Precarious Values: A Case Study." *American Sociological Review* 21(1956)327–36.

CLEVEN, W. A., and FIEDLER, F. E. "Interpersonal Perceptions of Open-Hearth Foremen and Steel Production." *Journal of Applied Psychology* 41(1956):312–14.

COHEN, A. R. "The Effect of Situational Structure and Individual Self-Esteem on Threat Oriented Reactions to Power." Doctoral dissertation, University of Michigan at Ann Arbor, 1953.

———. "Upward Communication in Experimentally Created Hierarchies." *Human Relations* 11(1958):41–53.

———. "Situational Structure, Self-Esteem, and Threat-Oriented Reactions to Power." In *Studies in Social Power*, edited by D. Cartwright. Ann Arbor: University of Michigan Institute for Social Research, 1959.

COHEN, M. D., and MARCH, J. G. *Leadership and Ambiguity.* New York: McGraw-Hill, 1974. Sponsored by the Carnegie Commission on Higher Education.

COLLANOS, P. A., and ANDERSON, L. R. "Effect of Perceived Expertness upon Creativity of Members of Brainstorming Groups." *Journal of Applied Psychology* 2(1969):159–63.

COX, C. M. *The Early Mental Traits of Three Hundred Geniuses.* Stanford: Stanford University Press, 1926.

CUSSLER, M. *The Woman Executive.* New York: Harcourt, Brace and World, 1958.

DAHL, R. A. "The Concepts of Power." *Behavioral Science* 2(1957):201–15.

DORNBUSCH, S. M., and SCOTT, W. R. *Evaluation and the Exercise of Authority: A Theory of Control Applied to Diverse Organizations.* San Francisco: Jossey-Bass, 1975.

EBLE, K. E. *The Art of Administration.* San Francisco: Jossey-Bass, 1978.

EDELMAN, M. *The Symbolic Uses of Politics.* Urbana: University of Illinois Press, 1964.

EDITORIAL PROJECTS FOR EDUCATION, INC. *The Impossible Job: A Special Report on What It Takes to Run a College These Days.* Washington, D.C.: Editorial Projects for Education, 1976.

FALBO, T. "Multidimensional Scaling of Power Strategies." *Journal of Personality and Social Psychology* 35(1957):537–47.

FIEDLER, F. E. "Assumed Similarity Measures and Predictors of Team Effectiveness." *Journal of Abnormal Social Psychology* 48(1954):381–88.

———. "The Influence of Leader-Keyman Relations on Combat Crew Effectiveness." *Journal of Abnormal Social Psychology* 51(1955):227–235.

———. "The Effect of Leadership and Cultural Heterogeneity on Group Performance: A Test of the Contingency Model." *Journal of Experimental Social Psychology* 2(1966):237–64.

———. *A Theory of Leadership Effectiveness.* New York: McGraw-Hill, 1967.

———. "Leadership Experience and Leader Performance: Another Hypothesis Shot to Hell." *Organizational Behavior and Human Performance* 5(1970):1–14.

———. *Personality, Motivational Systems, and Behavior of High and Low LPC Persons.* Seattle: University of Washington, Technical Report 70-12, 1970.

———, and MEUWESE, W. A. T. "Leaders' Contribution to Task Performance in Cohesive and Uncohesive Groups." *Journal of Abnormal Social Psychology* 67(1963):83–87.

———; MEUWESE, W. A. T.; and OONK, S. "An Exploratory Study of Group Creativity in Laboratory Tasks." *Acta Psychol., Amst.* 18(1961):100–19.

———; O'BRIEN, G. E.; and ILGEN, D. R. "The Effect of Leadership Style upon the Performance and Adjustment of Volunteer Teams Operating in Successful Foreign Environment." *Human Relations* 22(1969):503–14.

FISHER, J. L. "Of Testing, Truth and Ralph Nader." *The New York Times,* Feb. 18, 1980.

———, ed. *Presidential Leadership in Advancement Activities: New Directions for Institutional Advancement (#8).* San Francisco: Jossey-Bass, 1980.

FOA, U. G., AND FOA, E. B. *Societal Structures of the Mind.* Springfield: C. C. Thomas, 1975.

FODOR, E. M. "Disparagement by a Subordinate as an Influence on the Use of Power." *Journal of Applied Psychology* 59(1974):652–55.

FRENCH, J. R. P.; MORRISON, W.; and LEVINGER, G. "Coercive Power and Forces Affecting Conformity." *Journal of Abnormal Social Psychology* 61(1960):93–101.

———, and RAVEN, B. "The Bases of Social Power." In *Studies in Social Power,* edited by D. Cartwright. Ann Arbor: University of Michigan, Institute for Social Research, 1959.

———, and RAVEN, B. "The Bases of Social Power." In *Group Dynamics* (3rd ed.), edited by D. Cartright and A. Zander. New York: Harper & Row, 1968.

———, and SNYDER, R. "Leadership and Interpersonal Power," In *Studies in Social Power,* edited by D. Cartwright. Ann Arbor: University of Michigan, Institute for Social Research, 1959.

GHISELLI, E. E. "Intelligence and Managerial Success." *Psychol. Rep.* 12(1963):898.

GODFREY, E. P.; FIEDLER, F. E.; and HALL, D. M. *Boards, Management and Company Success.* Danville: Interstate, 1959.

GOODSTADT, B., and HJELLE, L. A. "Power to the Powerless." *Journal of Personality and Social Psychology* 27(1973):190–96.

GOTTHEIL, E., and VIELHABER, D. P. "Interaction of Leader and Squad Attributes Related to Performance of Military Squads." *Journal of Social Psychology* 68(1966):113–27.

HALL, J., and HAWKER, J. R. *Power Management Inventory.* The Woodlands, Texas: Teleometrics International, 1981.

HAMMARSKJOLD, D. *Markings.* Lawrence, Mass.: Merrimack Book Service, 1965.

HAWKER, J. R., and HALL, J. *The Development and Initial Validation of a Scale for Assessing Power Motivation.* The Woodlands, Texas: Teleometrics International, 1981.

HAWKINS, C. H. "A Study of Factors Mediating a Relationship Between Leader Rating Behavior and Group Productivity." *Dissertation Abstracts* 23(1962):733.

HECHINGER, F. M. "Leadership Arises as a College Issue." *The New York Times,* Oct. 19, 1982.

HENSHEL, H. B. "The President Stands Alone." *Harvard Business Review,* September/October(1971):37–45.

HESBURGH, T. M. "Presidential Leadership: The Keystone for Advancement." In *Presidential Leadership in Advancement Activities,* edited by J. L. Fisher. San Francisco: Jossey-Bass 1980.

HILL, W. The validation and extension of Fiedler's theory of leadership effectiveness. *Academic Management Journal* 12(1969): 33–47.

HOBBES, T. *Leviathan.* England: Penguin Books, 1968.

HODGKINSON, H. L. "Presidents and Campus Governance: A Research Profile." *Educational Record* 51(1970):159–66.

———, and MEETH, L. R., eds. *Power and Authority.* San Francisco: Jossey-Bass, 1976.

HUNT, J. G. "Fiedler's Leadership Contingency Model: An Empirical Test in Three Organizations." *Organizational Behavior and Human Performance* 67(1967):290–308.

HURWITZ, J. I.; ZANDER, A.F.; and HYMOVITCH, B. "Some Effects of Power on the Relations among Group Members." In *Group Dynamics,* edited by D. Cartwright and A. Zander. Evanston: Row, Peterson, 1953.

HUTCHINS, E. B., and FIEDLER, F. E. "Task-Oriented and Quasi-Therapeutic Role Functions of the Leader in a Small Military Group." *Sociometry* 23(1960):393–406.

IVERSON, M. A. "Personality Impression of Punitive Stimulus Persons of Differential Status." *Journal of Abnormal and Social Psychology* 68(1964):617–26.

JENKINS, W. D. "A Review of Leadership Studies with Particular Reference to Military Problems." *Psychological Bulletin* 44 (1947):54–79.

JONES, E. E. *Ingratiation.* New York: Appleton-Century-Crofts, 1964.

———; GERGEN, K. J.; GUMPERT, P.; and THIBAUT, J. W. "Some Conditions Affecting the Use of Ingratiation to Influence Performance Evaluation." *Journal of Personality and Social Psychology* 1 (1965):613–25.

JONES, R. E., and JONES, E. E. "Optimum Conformity as an Ingratiation Tactic." *Journal Pers.* 32 (1964):436–58.

JULIAN, J. W. "Leader and Group Behavior as Correlates of Adjustment and Performance in Negotiation Groups." *Dissertation Abstracts* 23(1) (1954):646.

———; HOLLANDER, E. P.; and REGULA, C. R. "Endorsement of the Group Spokesman as a Function of His Source of Authority, Competence and Success." *Journal of Personality and Social Psychology* 11(1969):42–49.

KATZ, D. "Patterns of Leadership." In *Handbook of Political Psychology,* edited by J. N. Knutson. San Francisco: Jossey-Bass, 1973.

KAUFFMAN, J. F. *At the Pleasure of the Board.* Washington, D.C.: American Council on Education, 1980.

KELMAN, H. C., and LAWRENCE, L. H. "Assignment of Responsibility in the Case of Lt. Calley." *Journal of Social Issues* 28 (1982):177–212.

KERR, C. Personal Conversation, 1980.

KIPNIS, D. *The Powerholders.* Chicago: The University of Chicago Press, 1976.

———, and VANDERVEER, R. "Ingratiation and the Use of Power." *Journal of Personality and Social Psychology* 26(1971):245–50.

———, and WAGNER, D. "Character Structure and Response to Leadership." *Journal of Experimental Research in Personality* 1 (1967):16–24.

KNUTSON, J. N., ed. *Handbook of Political Psychology.* San Francisco: Jossey-Bass, 1973.

KORDA, M. *Power: How to Get it, How to Use It.* New York: Ballantine, 1976.

KORMAN, A. K. "The Prediction of Managerial Performance: A Review." *Personnel Psychology* 21(1958):295–322.

LAWLER, E. E. *Pay and Organizational Effectiveness.* New York: McGraw-Hill, 1971.

LEHMAN, H. C. *Age and Achievement.* Princeton: Princeton University Press, 1953.

LENNER, J. H. "The Justice Motive: 'Equity' and Parity among Children." *Journal of Personality and Social Psychology* 29 (1974)539–45.

LUCHINS, A. S., and LUCHINS, E. H. "On Conformity with Judgments of a Majority or an Authority." *Journal of Social Psychology* 53 (1961):303–16.

MacEOIN, G. "Notre Dame's Father Hesburgh." *Change* 8(1976):45–51.

MACHIAVELLI, N. *The Prince.* New York: Mentor Books, 1952.

MANN, R. D. "A Review of the Relationships between Personality and Performance in Small Groups." *Psychological Bulletin* 56(1959):241–70.

MARTIN, HOMER, M.D. Personal conversation, 1982.

MATTHEWS, D. R. *The Social Background of Political Decision-Makers.* New York: Random House, 1954.

MAUSNER, B. "Studies in Social Interaction III. Effect of Variation in One Partner's Prestige on the Interaction of Observer Pairs." *Journal of Applied Psychology* 37(1953):391–93.

MAY, R. *Power and Innocence.* New York: Norton, 1972.

MAYHEW, L. B.; GLENN, J.R.,JR. "College and University Presidents: Roles in Transition." *Liberal Education* 61(1975):299–308.

McCLELLAND, D. C. "The Two Faces of Power." *Journal of International Affairs* 24(1969):141–54.

————. *Power: The Inner Experience.* New York: Irvington, 1975.

————, and BURNHAM, D. H. "Power Is the Great Motivator." *Harvard Business Review* 54(1976):100–10.

MECHANIC, D. "Sources of Power of Lower Participants in Complex Organizations." *Administrative Science Quarterly* 7(1962):349–364

MERTON, R. K. and KITT, A. S. "Contributions to the Theory of Reference Group Behavior." In *Studies in the Scope and Method of "The American Soldier,"* edited by R.K. Merton and P.R. Lazarfeld. Glencoe: Free Press, 1950.

MILGRAM, S. "Some Conditions of Obedience and Disobedience to Authority." *Human Relations* 18(1965):57,–76.

MILLER, R. I. *An Assessment of College Performance.* San Francisco: Jossey-Bass, 1979.

MILLS, T. M. "Power Relations in Three-Person Groups." *American Sociological Review* 18(1953):351–57.

MOTT, P. E. "Power, Authority and Influence." In *The Structure of Community Power,* edited by M. Aiken and P. E. Mott. New York: Random House, 1970.

MOYER, K. E. "The Physiology of Aggression and the Implications for Aggression Control." In *The Control of Aggression and Violence,* edited by J. L. Singer. New York: Academic Press, 1971.

MURDOCH, P. "Development of Contractual Norms in a Dyad." *Journal of Personality and Social Psychology* 6(1967):206–11.

NEUSTADT, R. E. *Presidential Power.* New York: John Wiley and Sons, 1960.

NEWCOMER, M. *The Big Business Executive: The Factors That Made Him, 1900–1950.* New York: Columbia University Press, 1955.

NISBET, R. A. *The Social Bond.* New York: Alfred A. Knopf, 1970.

PEAY, M. "The Effects of Social Power and Pre-Existing Attitudes on Public and Private Responses to an Induced Attitude." *Human Relations* 29(1976):1115–29.

PELZ, D. C. "Leadership within a Hierarchical Organization." *Journal of Social Issues* 7(1951)49–55.

PETERS, T. J. "Symbols, Patterns, and Settings: An Optimistic Case for Getting Things Done." *Organizational Dynamics* 7(1978):3–23.

PFEFFER, J. *Power in Organizations.* Marshfield: Pittman Publishing, Inc., 1981.

POWELL, R. M. *Race, Religion, and the Promotion of the American Executive.* Columbus: Ohio State University, College of Administrative Science, 1969.

PRAY, F. C. "The President as 'Reasonable Adventurer.'" *AGB Reports* May/June (1979):45–48 (Washington, D.C.: Association of Governing Boards).

PRUITT, G. A. *A Blueprint for Leadership: The American College Presidency.* (Doctoral dissertation) Union Graduate School (Ohio) 1974.

RAVEN, B. H. "The Comparative Analysis of Power and Influence." In *Perspectives on Social Power,* edited by J. T. Tedeschi. Chicago: Aldine, 1974.

————, and FRENCH, J. R. P. "An Experimental Investigation of Legitimate and Coercive Power." *American Psychologist* 12(1957):393.

————, and KRUGLANSKI, A. W. "Conflict and Power." In *The Structure of Conflict,* edited by P. Swingle. New York: Academic Press, 1970.

RICHMAN, B. M. and FARMER, R. N. *Leadership, Goals, and Power in Higher Education: A Contingency and Open-System Approach to Effective Management.* San Francisco: Jossey-Bass, 1974.

RIESMAN, D. "Beyond the '60s." *Wilson Quarterly* II(1978):59–71.

————. Personal conversation, 1980.

RUBIN, I. M. and GOLDMAN, M. "An Open System Model of Leadership Performance." *Organizational Behavior and Human Performance* 3(1968):143–56.

RUSSELL, B. *Power.* London: Allen and Urwin, 1938.

SCHELL, D. W. "Effect of Machiavellian Orientation and Intraorganization Power on Resource Allocation in Reorganization Coalitions: An Experimental Approach." Doctoral dissertation, Indiana University Graduate School of Business, 1970.

SCHLESINGER, A. M., JR. *The Age of Roosevelt,* vol. 2: *The Coming of the New Deal.* Boston: Houghton Mifflin, 1959.

Scientific American. "The Big Business Executive: 1964," 1965.

SCOTT, E. L. *Leadership and Perceptions of Organization.* Columbus: Ohio State University Bureau of Business Research, 1956.

SEEMAN, M. *Social Status and Leadership—The Case of the School Executive.* Columbus: Ohio State University, Educational Research Monograph No. 35, 1960.

SHAW, E. P. "The Social Distance Factor and Management." *Personnel Administration* 28(1965):29–31.

SHEPHERD, C., and WESCHLER, I. R. "The Relationship between Three Interpersonal Variables and Communication Effectiveness: A Pilot Study." *Sociometry* 18(1955):103–10.

SHRIVER, B. "The Behavioral Effects of Changes in Ascribed Leadership Status in Small Groups." Doctoral dissertation, University of Rochester, 1952.

SIU, R. G. H. *The Craft of Power*. New York: John Wiley and Sons, 1979.

SLUSHER, E. A.; ROSE, G. L.; and ROERING, K. J. "Commitment of Future Interaction and Relative Power under Conditions of Interdependence." *Journal of Conflict Resolution* 22(1978):282–98.

SMITH, P. B. *Groups within Organizations*. New York: Harper and Row, 1973.

STANDARD AND POORS. *Register of Corporations, Directors, and Executives*. New York: Standard and Poors, 1967.

STEERS, R. M. *Introduction to Organizational Behavior*. Santa Monica: Goodyear, 1981.

STOGDILL, R. M. "Personal Factors Associated with Leadership: A Survey of the Literature." *Journal of Psychology* 25(1948):35–71.

————. *Handbook of Leadership*. New York: Macmillan, 1974.

STOKE, H. W. *The American College President*. New York: Harper and Brothers, 1959.

STOTLAND, E. "Peer Groups and Reaction to Power Figures." In *Studies in Social Power*, edited by D. Cartwright. Ann Arbor: University of Michigan, Institute for Social Research, 1959.

STUDENT, K. R. "Supervisory Influence and Work-Group Performance." *Journal of Applied Psychology* 52(1968):188–94.

SWINGLE, P. "Exploitative Behavior in Non-Zero-Sum Games." *Journal of Personality and Social Psychology* 16(1970)121–32.

————, ed. *The Structure of Conflict*. New York: Academic Press, 1970.

TEDESCHI, J. T.; LINDSKOLD, S.; HORAI, J.; and GAHAGAN, J. P. "Social Power and the Credibility of Promises." *Journal of Personality and Social Psychology* 13(1969):253–61.

TEDESCHI, J. T.; SCHLENKER, B. R.; and BONOMA, T. B. "Cognitive Dissonance: Private Ratiocination or Private Spectacle." *American Psychologist* 26(1972):685–95.

————. *Conflict, Power and Games*. Chicago: Aldine, 1973.

THIAGARAJAN, K. M., and DEEP, S. D. "A Study of Supervisor-Subordinate Influence and Satisfaction in Four Cultures." *Journal of Social Psychology* 82(1970):173–80.

THIBAUT, J. W., and GRUDER, C. L. "Formation of Contractual Agreements Between Parties of Unequal Power." *Journal of Personality and Social Psychology* 11(1969):59–65.

TORRANCE, E. P. *Some Consequences of Power Differences on Decisions in B-26 Crews.* San Antonio: USAF Personnel and Training Research Center, Research Bulletin 54-128, 1954.

———. "Some Consequences of Power Differences in Permanent and Temporary Three-Man Groups." In *Small Groups,* edited by P. Hane, E. F. Borgatta, and R. F. Baers. New York: Knopf, 1955.

———. "The Influence of Experienced Members of Small Groups on the Behavior of the Inexperienced." *Journal of Social Psychology* 49(1959):249–57.

———. "A Theory of Leadership and Interpersonal Behavior." In *Leadership and Interpersonal Behavior,* edited by L. Petrullo and B. Bass. New York: Holt, Rinehart and Winston, 1961.

———, and ALIOTTI, N. C. "Accuracy, Task Effectiveness, and Emergence of a Social-Emotional Resolver as a Function of One- and Two-Expert Groups." *Journal of Psychology* 61(1965):161–70.

———, and MASON, R. "The Indigenous Leader in Changing Attitudes and Behavior." *International Journal of Sociometry* 1(1956):23–28.

VEYSEY, L. R. *The Emergence of the American University.* Chicago: University of Chicago Press, 1965.

WALKER, D. E. *The Effective Administrator.* San Francisco: Jossey-Bass, 1979.

WEBER, M. *The Theory of Social and Economic Organization.* Translated by M. Henderson and T. Parsons. New York: Oxford University Press, 1947.

ZANDER, A. "The Effects of Prestige on the Behavior of Group Members: An Audience Demonstration." *American Management Association, Personnel Service,* No. 155, 1953.

———, and COHEN, A. R. "Attributed Social Power and Group Acceptance: A Classroom Experimental Demonstration." *Journal of Abnormal Social Psychology* 51(1955):490–92.

————, and CURTIS, T. "Effects of Social Power on Aspiration Setting and Striving." *Journal of Abnormal Social Psychology* 64(1962):63–74.

Index